Susanna

Wesley

Her Remarkable Life

Susanna Wesley

Her Remarkable Life

by Ray Comfort with Trisha Ramos

BRIDGE
LOGOS

Alachua, Florida 32615

Bridge-Logos
Alachua, FL 32615 USA

Susanna Wesley: Her Remarkable Life
Ray Comfort with Trisha Ramos

Unless otherwise indicated, the Scripture quotations in this publication are taken from the King James Version of the Bible.

Printed in the United States of America.

Library of Congress Catalog Card Number: 2014953405
International Standard Book Number 978-1-61036-135-4

BP 09-09-15

SPECIAL THANKS

THANK YOU to Kristen Rasor for her editorial research and her labor to make sure every word made sense. We really appreciate you volunteering your time and effort on this project. Thank you also to Bridge-Logos for pitching this idea and for your years of faithfulness in allowing our friendship via publishing to continue—and for keeping the memories alive of so many that, like Susanna, have gone to be with the Lord.

CONTENTS

A Word to the Reader

G ODLY WOMEN in the New Testament are given great honor by the apostles and by Jesus Himself. Throughout the history of the Church, from the time of the New Testament, through the Reformation era and Puritan divines, and even today, women have exemplified Godly values. These women are prime examples of holiness and wisdom in their conduct at home, in raising children, caring for their husbands, taking in the poor and needy, buying and selling, and living their lives in the fear of God. Some of these precious women have even suffered martyrdom for the sake of Christ; others have laid down their lives for their families. Susanna Wesley is numbered among these incredible women in the history of the Church.

History tells us that just a few years before Susanna was born, the Great Plague killed an estimated 100,000 people; this number was about 15 percent of the population of London. To set the stage even more for her dramatic life, the Great Fire of London occurred just three years before Susanna was born.

Imagine what life with nineteen kids would have been like in the late sixteen-hundreds, especially if you live in America, where many tend to believe that 2.5 kids or fewer is acceptable and anything more can get you looks at the store. One wonders what sort of looks Susanna Wesley would have received in the marketplace, where people knew that she had given birth to nineteen children and had lost all but ten.

Susanna didn't have all the luxuries that families do today. She couldn't simply throw the children's clothes in the washer and let it do all the work while she tended to her other duties. She didn't have bottled water from the store, or a doctor who was just a phone call away. There were no phones!

What was life like for Susanna? What else does history tell us? What sort of family was she raised in? Who were her parents? What kind of conditions did she grow up in? What were her views on marriage and raising children? When did she get saved? What was it like being married to Samuel Wesley? What about her famous sons, Charles and John Wesley, founders of the Methodist Church? And how can we learn today from her example?

Because Susanna was greatly influenced by the Puritans, several chapters of this book will close with Puritan prayers taken from *The Valley of Vision: A Collection of Puritan Prayers and Devotions*.[1] It is very probable that many of these prayers she prayed herself.

Our hope is that you will glean from reading about the good, the bad, and the not-so-pretty times of Susanna's life, and that this book will cause you to seek the Lord in a deeper way through study, prayer, and meditation. May it help you grow in your personal sanctification and in the knowledge of our Lord Jesus Christ.

CHAPTER 1
SUSANNA'S LIFE GROWING UP

SUSANNA ANNESLEY WESLEY was born on January 20, 1669 in London (Spital Yard, Bishopsgate) to Mary (White) and Samuel Annesley. Samuel Annesley was a Nonconformist minister who was greatly respected among his fellow Puritans. Susanna was their youngest child: number *twenty-five*.

One of Susanna's early biographers recorded the following conversation:

'How many children has Doctor Annesley?' said a friend to Thomas Manton, who had just consecrated one more to the Lord in the Holy Sacrament of Baptism. 'I believe it is two dozen, or a quarter of a hundred' was the startling reply. 'This reckoning children by dozens', sagely remarks the eccentric John Dunton, 'is a singular circumstance; an honour to which few persons ever arrive.' Is it possible to catch a glimpse of this 'quarter of a hundred' children of one family, and for some definite idea of the home circle in which Susanna Wesley passed her years? Records largely fail us, and the task can be only partially performed. Many of them, probably, were but 'sons of a night,' and, like early spring flowers, withered away the moment life's morning sunbeams began to beat upon their head. Others bloomed into youthful beauty; and a few developed into mature life."[1]

Susanna's life was anything but normal, and her future was far from ordinary. She played a very important part in Church history as she later ended up marrying Samuel Wesley, bearing nineteen children (losing nine of them to early deaths), and from the ten who remained, raising two of them, John and Charles, to become incredible evangelists, hymn-writers, and the founders of Methodism. Because of this, Susanna has been called by many "the Mother of Methodism."

Susanna was very close with her father. They had many things in common, including a love of books and a deep interest in theological talks (which began at a very young age). The Reverend Samuel Annesley "was a man of noteworthy character":

> Born of devout Puritan parents, he stated that he was so early instructed in the way of salvation that he could not remember a time when he was conscious of not knowing the Lord. At the age of five he began to read twenty chapters of the Bible a day and this practice he continued till the close of his life. Early in his teens he entered Oxford University and upon graduating in 1644 he was ordained and became the pastor of a church in the county of Kent.[2]

Susanna had a very independent spirit. While all the other children were outside playing, she wanted to be inside reading. When the day outside was nice and sunny, Susanna's sister Elizabeth, (who called her Sukey) would scold her, saying, "Sukey, the weather is much too fine to hide from!"[3] Still, she would rather be talking theology with her father in the library or have her nose in a theological book.

Susanna longed for wisdom. She had a brilliant mind, and her well-learned and intelligent father was eager to teach her, opening his huge library for her to explore for herself.

All of London called the Annesley sisters pretty.[4] Susanna, who was the youngest, was said to have been the prettiest of all, and people complimented her for her dark silky hair and her beautiful blue eyes. As she grew into a young woman, she was not only pretty, but also very well-learned. She could read Hebrew, Latin, and Greek, and could hold her own in discussing theology with seminarians.[5]

Susanna's father's personal appearance was noble and commanding. To describe him, his contemporaries used phrases such as "fine figure," "dignified man," "highly expressive and amiable countenance." Susanna Wesley's biographer John Kirk wrote of Samuel Annesley:

> Hardy in constitution and almost insensible to cold, a hat, gloves, and topcoat were of no necessity to him, even in the depth of winter.
>
> The days of "hoare frost" and chilling winds found him in his study, at the top of the house, with open window and empty fire-grate. Temperate in all things, he needed no stimulants, and from his infancy hardly ever drank any thing but water.
>
> He could endure any amount of active exercise and toil, preaching "twice or thrice every day of the week" without any sense of weariness. Till the time that the Divine Voice said unto him, "Get thee up and die," his eye was not dim, nor his natural force abated.[6]

It was said of him:

"He lived in the unclouded light of the divine countenance," Many called him "the instrument of their conversion" and "during the next quarter of a century he was one of the most attractive, laborious and useful preachers of his day." The forces of nonconformity looked upon him as their most prominent figure and their leader.[7]

The Annesley's daughter, Elizabeth, spoke about her parents in her writings and acknowledged "in her papers, found after her death, the good providence of God in giving her religious parents, that, with united endeavors, took a mighty care of her education."[8]

Susanna's mother, Mary, appears to have been a person of great strength and character. Samuel Annesley's first wife had died at the birth of their first child. The widower married this second wife, who bore him the other twenty-four children, several of whom died in infancy.

> Thomas Doolittle, a Nonconformist minister who lived during the time of Susanna, had a high view of the family when he said, "Masters of families ought to read the Scripture to their families and instruct their children and servants in the matters and doctrines of salvation. Therefore, they are to pray in and with their families."

Although not much is known about Mary, the following was written about her:

The few dim intimations concerning her impress us with the idea that she was a woman of superior

4

understanding and earnest and constant purity. She spared no labour in endeavouring to promote the religious welfare of her numerous children. She must also have been hard-working and endowed with remarkable patience, to have borne and brought up so large a family.[9]

Samuel Annesley had many strong convictions that were clearly seen during his first pastorate in the county of Kent. The previous pastor had taken more liberties, but Samuel didn't want anything to do with such worldly behavior. Apparently, the congregation tried to persecute them and he said, "Use me as you will, I am resolved to continue with you til God has fitted you, by my ministry, to entertain a better man."[10] His commitment to the people continued until he saw a change in their practices and he moved to London.

His times in London were not easy. London is where he refused, in 1662, to submit to the Church of England, whose latest mission was to stamp out Puritanism. Toward this end, Parliament passed the Act of Uniformity, which commanded all ministers to conform to all beliefs and

Pilgrim's Progress, written from a prison cell, sold more than 100,000 copies within John Bunyan's lifetime. Up to the present day, it is believed to be the second most widely distributed book in the world, surpassed only by the Bible itself. Never out of print, it has been translated into over two hundred languages.

practices of the Church of England. Approximately two thousand men refused to submit, and these men were thereafter called Nonconformists or Dissenters. The famous writer John Bunyan, who penned *The Pilgrim's Progress,* suffered in prison as a result of this law. Sadly, many were driven out of their ministry positions, from their churches, and out of universities, an event which became known as "the Great Ejection." Many of these men were not allowed to preach, and often they and their families faced poverty and even homelessness because of their strong beliefs.

Samuel Annseley was one of the leading men out of the two thousand who stood up against the Church of England, but his stance was costly. Biographer Dallimore tells about it:

> Among the holiest and best of this large band of confessors, was Samuel Annesley. His relative, Lord Anglesea, then in high favour with the ruling powers, used efforts to induce him to conform, and probably offered him high preferment if he remained in the Establishment. But, he would not yield; and at no small cost. . . .[11]

Literally, his convictions cost him: seven hundred pounds a year.[12] The kind of oppression he lived under is difficult to imagine. All of his comings and goings were under scrutiny. Dallimore continues:

> His activities were constantly watched by the Royalist officials, and although he was never arrested, on one occasion, on which an officer suddenly fell to the floor, dead, in the very act of signing a warrant for his arrest. But the danger of being seized and thrown into prison was always hanging over him and must have been a constant strain on his wife and family, as well as himself.[13]

While Susanna's father Samuel was serving as

minister of a nonconformist meeting house located in London (Little St. Helen's Place), the family lived in a nice district on a street called Spital Yard. This street consisted of decent homes, and this is the home where all of the children grew up. (We do not know the names of all the twenty-five children of Samuel and Mary Annesley, but seven of the twenty-five have been recorded: Samuel, Benjamin, Judith, Anne, Elizabeth, Sarah, and the youngest of the family, Susanna).

So, this is the backdrop for Susanna's childhood years: high tension because of religious persecution, a gigantic family with plenty of needs to be taken care of, and attentive parents. As far as we know, even though her father was continually harassed by authorities, he did not become agitated or unsettled; he remained restrained as he tended to his many responsibilities, thus earning respect from outsiders.

Apparently at one time during her childhood, Susanna was saved from death. We have her written mention of "preservation from ill accidents and once from a violent death."[14] Nobody knows what happened to her. It could have been a fire from a large open fireplace or a fallen candle or an accident with a horse; what we do know is that God spared her life, because it was not yet her time to die.

> [Susanna] had strict rules for her personal life and for the lives of her own children. In a letter to her son, John Wesley, many years later, she stated, "I will tell you what rule I observed . . . when I was young, and too much addicted to childish diversions, which was this—never to spend more time in mere recreation in one day than I spent in private religious devotions."

Universities did not yet enroll women when Susanna

was growing up. But even without having the luxury of attending a university as women do today, she was exceptionally well-educated for her day.

Susanna was the kind of person who would never give a second thought to even the best of the literature that had been produced by the Restoration authors, but with her father's library available she undoubtedly read "certain books of the Reformers and the Puritans, difficult as their works would seem for a young girl to read."[15]

She had a definite mind of her own, and the evidence of her very opinionated spirit is the fact that, while not yet thirteen years old, she decided to separate from the Nonconformists and join the established Church of England, the very church that had brought so much pain to her family. Later, in 1709, she wrote, "I had drawn up an account of the whole transaction," and later in life she wrote to her oldest son, ". . . under which head I had included the main of the controversy between them and the Established Church, as far as it had come to my knowledge; and then followed the reasons that determined my judgment to the preference of the Church of England"[16]

Many have speculated as to when Susanna came to the Lord, but history does not make it clear. Some think she was converted as a young girl while living in her father's home. But "two years before she died she had an experience which her sons Charles and John regarded as her conversion."[17] In fact, John and Charles Wesley seemed to think her whole life up to that moment was lived under legalism and rules, and that it did not necessarily reflect true conversion. Still, others would disagree with their assessment, saying that she bore the marks of a genuine convert for many years. (This issue will be discussed more in chapter 7, "Susanna's Conversion— True or False?")

CHAPTER 2
PURITANS IN HER HOME

D URING SUSANNA'S CHILDHOOD, the Annesley home was visited by several great Puritan writers. Richard Baxter, John Owen, and Thomas Manton were just a few who walked through their doors. Manton was the minister who baptized Susanna. In her own home, Susanna heard the discussions of the Puritan leaders and their arguments against the Church of England.

The following list is a small sample of the Puritans that were friends with Susanna's father Samuel, who either visited their home or preached with him:

John Owen (1616–1683. Famous for his book, *Communion with God*)

Richard Baxter (1615–1691. Famous for writing *A Call to the Unconverted to Turn and Live*)

Thomas Watson (1620–1686. Famous for writing *All Things for Good*)

John Bunyan (1628–1688. Famous imprisoned author of *The Pilgrims Progress*)

Stephen Charnock (1628–1680. Famous for writing *The Existence and Attributes of God*)

Thomas Manton (1620–1677. Famous for his exposition of the book of James)

Thomas Boston (1676–1732. Famous for his book, *The Art of Man-Fishing*)

Susanna's father came from a devout Puritan family, and he said he could not remember not knowing the Lord. His parents worked hard to instill in him a Puritan passion for holiness and upright living. Not wasting any time, they started discipling him at a very young age, and at just five years old he began reading twenty chapters of the Bible a day. As an adult, Samuel Annesley was known not only for his devotion to the Lord, but also for his outgoing personality and charisma, and he was seen as one of the great leaders of the Puritans. He was very well-educated and he had quite an expensive library. All of this had a great influence on Susanna as she grew up.

In her father's home, Susanna would have met a member of her father's congregation named Daniel Defoe, the man who later wrote the novel, *Robinson Crusoe*. He was about ten years older than Susanna.

An outgrowth of the Protestant Reformation, Puritanism stressed the importance of conscience as arbiter of an individual's actions. Susanna's Puritan father Samuel often preached on freedom of conscience; and she certainly inherited his independence of mind and his willingness to dissent from religious practices when doing so bothered her conscience.

Susanna's father corresponded often with Puritan John Owen. Here is a brief quote from a foreword they wrote together for a book on the doctrines of grace:

> There are some very important advantages which come out of this study. First, that it is founded and built on the testimony of God alone whose authority and truth are the only perfect rule and immoveable

basis of divine faith. It is its best benchmark. Secondly, that the doctrines being declared and vindicated here is through the best use of them to excite and influence our hearts and lives according to the genuine tenor and import of those truths. This is in opposition to what the contrary doctrines have ever pretended to be themselves. It may be a supplement to other books, where the same truths are worthily contended for, but may be defective in this application of the truths to the Christian life. So, it is not only a work of good use in and of itself, but it also rescues these doctrines from one of the worst scandals that they have been derogated in. Various other reasons might be mentioned for reading this study. We could say many more things that are of help. But, for brevity's sake, the reader is referred to his good sense while reading the book.

We hope that the book may be entertained by men according to its deserts, and blessed of God in the ends it is designed and suited to, is, and shall be the desire of,

John Owen & Samuel Annesley[1]

Here are some encouraging, thought-provoking, and convicting quotes from some of the well-known Puritans who came to visit Susanna's home when she was young. She very well could have heard words such as these spoken by their own lips:

JOHN OWEN:

Labour to grow better under all your afflictions, lest your afflictions grow worse, lest God mingle them with more darkness, bitterness and terror.

We cannot enjoy peace in this world unless we are ready to yield to the will of God in respect of death. Our times are in His hand, at His sovereign disposal. We must accept that as best.

Love precedes discipline.

The foundation of true holiness and true Christian worship is the doctrine of the gospel, what we are to believe. So when Christian doctrine is neglected, forsaken, or corrupted, true holiness and worship will also be neglected, forsaken, and corrupted.

Poor souls are apt to think that all those whom they read of or hear of to be gone to heaven, went thither because they were so good and so holy. Yet not one of them, not any man that is now in heaven (Jesus Christ alone excepted), did ever come thither any other way but by forgiveness of sins. And that will also bring us higher, though we come short of many of them in holiness and grace.

When someone acts weak, negligent, or casual in a duty—performing it carelessly or lifelessly, without any genuine satisfaction, joy, or interest—he has already entered into the spirit that will lead him into trouble. How many we see today who have departed from warmhearted service and have become negligent, careless, and indifferent in their prayer life or in the reading of the Scriptures. For each one who escapes this peril, a hundred others will be ensnared. Then it may be too late to acknowledge, "I neglected private prayer," or "I did not meditate on God's Word," or "I did not hear what I should have listened to."

A minister may fill his pews, his communion roll, the mouths of the public, but what that minister is on his knees in secret before God Almighty, that he is and no more.

If we do not abide in prayer, we will abide in temptation. Let this be one aspect of our daily intercession: "God, preserve my soul, and keep my heart and all its ways so that I will not be entangled." When this is true in our lives, a passing temptation will not overcome us. We will remain free while others lie in bondage.

If we would talk less and pray more about them, things would be better than they are in the world: at least, we should be better enabled to bear them.

He who prays as he ought, will endeavor to live as he prays.

We ought as much to pray for a blessing upon our daily rod as upon our daily bread.

RICHARD BAXTER:

An ounce of mirth is worth a pound of sorrow.

Sometimes trouble helps a person turn to God. Sickness says, "See if your wealth or pleasures can help you! Can they keep your departing soul in your

15

body? Cry aloud to them, and see if they can substitute for God!" O, how this gets through to the sinner. Common sense admits the truth, and even the flesh is convinced of its own insufficiency.

Spend your time in nothing which you know must be repented of; in nothing on which you might not pray for the blessing of God; in nothing which you could not review with a quiet conscience on your dying bed; in nothing which you might not safely and properly be found doing if death should surprise you in the act.

> While some ministers were wrangling about the divine right of Episcopacy or Presbytery, or splitting hairs about reprobation and free-will, Baxter was always visiting from house to house and beseeching men for Christ's sake, to be reconciled to God. . . . While others were entangling themselves in politics, and "burying their dead" amidst the potsherds of the earth, Baxter was living a crucified life and daily preaching the Gospel.[2]
> —J.C. Ryle

You may know God, but not comprehend Him.

Prayer is the breath of the new creature.

Prayer must carry on our work, as well as preaching. He does not preach heartily to his people who does not pray for them. If we do not prevail with God to give them repentance and faith, we are not likely to prevail with them to repent and believe.

> Richard Baxter once preached, "Let God have your first awaking thoughts; lift up your hearts to Him reverently and thankfully for the rest enjoyed the night before, and cast yourself upon Him for the day which follows."[3]

This life was not intended to be the place of our perfection, but the preparation for it.

THOMAS WATSON:

A wicked man in prayer may lift up his hands, but he cannot lift up his face.

The prayer that is faithless is fruitless.

Prayer is the soul's breathing itself into the bosom of its heavenly Father.

The angel fetched Peter out of prison, but it was prayer that fetched the angel.

A spiritual prayer is a humble prayer. Prayer is the asking of an alms, which requires humility. . . . The lower the heart descends, the higher the prayer ascends.

If there is anything excellent, it is salvation; if there be anything necessary, it is working out salvation; if there be any tool to work with, tis holy fear.

Adoption is a greater mercy than Adam had in paradise.

What if we have more of the rough file, if we have less rust! Afflictions carry away nothing but the dross of sin.

Afflictions add to the saints' glory. The more the diamond is cut, the more it sparkles; the heavier the saints' cross is, the heavier will be their crown.

Affliction may be lasting, but it is not everlasting. Affliction was a sting, but withal a wing: sorrow shall soon fly away.

To obey God in some things, and not in others, shows an unsound heart. Childlike obedience moves toward even command of God, as the needle points where the loadstone draws.

A child of God, though he cannot serve the Lord perfectly, yet he serves him willingly; his will is in the law of the Lord; he is not a pressed soldier, but a volunteer. By the beating of this pulse we may judge whether there be spiritual life in us or no.

Be not only attentive in hearing, but retentive after hearing.

JOHN BUNYAN:

In prayer it is better to have a heart without words than words without a heart.

Prayer will make a man cease from sin, or sin will entice a man to cease from prayer.

What God says is best, is best, though all the men in the world are against it.

I will stay in prison till the moss grows on my eye lids rather than disobey God.

One leak will sink a ship, and one sin will destroy a sinner.

He who runs from God in the morning will scarcely find Him the rest of the day.

STEPHEN CHARNOCK:

All the prayers in the Scripture you will find to be reasoning with God, not a multitude of words heaped together.

In regard of God, patience is a submission to His sovereignty. To endure a trial, simply because we cannot avoid or resist it, is not Christian patience. But to humbly submit because it is the will of God to inflict the trial, to be silent because the sovereignty of God orders it—is true godly patience.

Without faith we are not fit to desire mercy, without humility we are not fit to receive it, without affection we are not fit to value it, without sincerity we are not fit to improve it. Times of extremity contribute to the growth and exercise of these qualifications.

Since nothing but God is eternal, nothing but God is worth the loving.

We often learn more of God under the rod that strikes us than under the staff that comforts us.

If God is in fact our Enemy with only destructive intentions toward us, why do we experience any good at all? It isn't surprising that life is painful. What's surprising is that life is joyful. What do our simple, daily joys mean? Is God pretending to be our Friend, is He setting us up for the ultimate nasty surprise? Or is God sending us signals every day that His heart is loving and kind, so kind that we can go back to Him in repentance and find His arms open to us?

THOMAS MANTON:

One way to get comfort is to plead the promise of God in prayer, show Him His handwriting; God is tender of His Word.

Faith is the fountain of prayer, and prayer should be nothing else but faith exercised.

First we practice sin, then defend it, then boast of it.

If a man would lead a happy life, let him but seek a sure object for his trust, and he shall be safe: "He shall not be afraid of evil tidings: his heart is fixed, trusting in the Lord." He hath laid up his confidence in God, therefore his heart is kept in an equal poise.

Continued meditation brings great profit to the soul. Passant and transient thoughts are more pleasant, but not so profitable. Deliberate meditation is of most use because it secures the return of the thoughts.

The end of study is information, and the end of meditation is practice, or a work upon the affections. Study is like a winter sun that shines, but warms not: but meditation is like a blowing upon the fire, where we do not mind the blaze, but the heat. The end of study is to hoard up truth; but of meditation to lay it forth in conference or holy conversation.

What is the reason there is so much preaching and so little practice? For want of meditation . . . Constant thoughts are operative, and musing makes the fire burn. Green wood is not kindled by a flash or spark, but by constant blowing.

THOMAS BOSTON:

A righteous man may make a righteous work, but no work of an unrighteous man can make him righteous. Now we become righteous only by faith, through the righteousness of Christ imputed to us.

A man shall as soon force fruit out of a branch broken off from the tree and withered, as work righteousness without believing in, and uniting with Christ. These are two things by which those that hear the gospel are ruined.

It is great folly to cast your sins upon Satan who tempted you, or upon your neighbor who provoked you; but it is a far greater sin, nay horrid blasphemy, to cast it upon God Himself. A greater affront than this cannot be offered to the infinite holiness of God.

For as the sun darts its beams upon a dunghill, and yet is no way defiled by it; so God decrees the permission of sin . . . yet is not the author of sin.

God hath decreed the end, so He hath decreed the means that are proper for attaining that end; so that these two must not be separated.

PURITAN PRAYER[4]

O Sovereign Lord, thou art the Creator-Father of all men, for thou hast made and dost support them; thou art the special Father of those who know, love and honour thee, who find thy yoke easy, and thy burden light, thy work honourable, thy commandments glorious. But how little thy undeserved goodness has affected me! how imperfectly have I improved my religious privileges! how negligent have I been in doing good to others! I am before thee in my trespasses and sins, have mercy on me, and may thy goodness bring me to repentance. Help me to hate and forsake every false way, to be attentive to my condition and character, to bridle my tongue, to keep my heart with all diligence, to watch and pray against temptation, to mortify sin, to be concerned for the salvation of others. O God, I cannot endure to see the destruction of my kindred. Let those that are united to me in tender ties be precious in thy sight and devoted to thy glory. Sanctify and prosper my domestic devotion, instruction, discipline, example, that my house may be a nursery for heaven, my church the garden of the Lord, enriched with trees of righteousness of thy planting, for thy glory; Let not those of my family who are amiable, moral, attractive, fall short of heaven at last; Grant that the promising appearances of a tender conscience, soft heart, the alarms and delights of thy Word, be not finally blotted out, but bring forth judgment unto victory in all whom I love. Amen.

CHAPTER 3
SUSANNA MEETS PRINCE CHARMING

ONE CAN IMAGINE that with twenty-five children and a father as famous as Samuel Annesley, Susanna's home had a continual revolving door. Besides Puritans such as Richard Baxter, Thomas Manton, and John Owen visiting their home, many students were very drawn to Dr. Annesley's wisdom and knowledge (one would also assume that, since he had such attractive daughters, some of the students may have had ulterior motives in mind).

One regular visitor was John Dunton, who became a noted publisher. The first time he entered Dr. Annesley's church, he said that:

"... instead of engaging my attention to what the Doctor said, I suffered my mind and my eyes to run at random. I soon singled out a young lady who almost charmed me mad." This was one of the Annesley girls, but to Dunton's immense displeasure she proved to be already engaged. But he quickly took up with her sister Elizabeth and became equally enthralled with her.[1]

Months later, Dunton and Susanna's sister Elizabeth were married. At the wedding was Samuel Wesley, who happened to be one of John Dunton's close friends. He even spoke at the wedding and read a poem that had a romantic air. Perhaps this is what first drew Susanna in, and perhaps this is the first time she saw him. Samuel was older than thirteen-year-old Susanna by six years, making him nineteen at this time. However, she was very mature for her age as she had already left the dissenting group and voiced her approval of the Church of England. "There is reason to believe that a firm friendship sprang up between them at about this time. It is particularly significant that, just as Susanna had left the Dissenters and had joined the Church of England, so Samuel also now prepared to take the same step."[2]

That these two shared the same views is very interesting, because Samuel's father, John Wesley, like Samuel Annesley, was a Nonconformist minister; his move no doubt would have been disheartening for his father. Not only was his father from the dissenting group, but also his grandfather, Bartholomew Wesley, had been persecuted for his preaching by the Church of England in an attempt to silence him. Therefore, in the experience of both of these young people, all gody men were of Puritan thought and persuasion.

Samuel's grandfather, Bartholomew, had been both persecuted and honored:

> Driven from his living immediately after the Restoration [i.e., in the1660s], he practiced medicine for a livelihood; preaching whenever a safe opportunity presented itself; and honoured for his blameless character, sincere piety, and many domestic virtues. The place of his birth; the character of his boyhood; the home and changing scenes of his declining years; the spot where he found a grave to hide him from the fiery trials through which he had passed, are buried in oblivion. "He lived several years after he was silenced," says [vicar and friend of the Wesley

family] Calamy; "but the death of his son [John, Samuel's father],"— the only member of his family of whom we have any account,— "made a sensible alteration in him; so that he afterward declined apace, and did not long survive him."[3]

Samuel Wesley
(1662–1735)

Bartholomew's son, John Wesley (Samuel's father), was an evangelist. He preached in many cities and served as the pastor of a church in 1658. However, he was imprisoned for not using the Book of Common Prayer and was released in 1662, after which he continued fervently to preach in small gatherings. Samuel's father John "was educated with the greatest religious care, he had 'a very humbling sense of sin and a serious concern for salvation,' even while a school-boy."[4] He died at a relatively young age as a result of one of his imprisonments:

> He was arrested three times, served the sentence each time and was released, but during a fourth incarceration, in which he was forced to sleep on the cold bare earth of the loathsome prison, he fell ill and soon died. He was only forty-two, a martyr for the Dissenting cause.[5]

Samuel's father John had a lot of influence among very eminent Puritans, and he influenced his son's life greatly. At Oxford, Puritan Thomas Goodwin had formed "a Gathered Church," and among the colleagues, John Wesley was noted for his piety, even in the midst of other students who were very godly such as John Howe, Stephen Charnock, and John Owen, the vice-chancellor of the university.

So, like Susanna Annesley, Samuel Wesley had grown up under the very godly instruction of his father John and the teachings of the Dissenters.

Samuel's mother came from a very influential family as well. Her father was a member of the committee that produced the *Westminster Confession of Faith*. She also was the niece of the prominent historian, Dr. Thomas Fuller. In his book on Susanna Wesley, Arnold Dallimer writes that after ". . . only a few years of married life, this woman suffered [a] long period of homelessness to which she added the pain of losing her husband. Very little is known about her life at the time, but twenty years later we find her living in poverty in London and maintained by the kindness of her sons."[6]

While Samuel was young, he was cared for by friends among the Dissenters who thought well of him and recognized his great academic abilities. He attended a Dissenting academy and during that time he learned classical studies, "but he was also impulsive and quick-tempered and he confessed that he 'had a narrow escape from debauchery and ruin.'"[7] And, because Dissenters were not allowed to graduate from universities, furthering his education may have been one of his motives for joining the Church of England. Being a member of the Church of England would have allowed him to go to Oxford. It is safe to assume that he had higher aspirations for scholarly grandeur than he thought the Dissenters would allow him to achieve.

After joining the Church of England, Samuel attended Oxford, and he ended up being ordained in the Church of

England and spending the rest of his life in ministry. But his education was costly and he did not have parents to support him, as his father had already passed away and his mother was poverty-ridden. Dallimore records the details:

> Samuel had already incurred debts, but he accepted a grant of £30 from a Dissenting fund and paid what he owed. Then, since he lived with his mother and knew his action would severely distress her, he said nothing about his intentions. Instead, he got up very early one morning and, carrying his earthly possessions in a bag slung over his shoulder, he "footed it" to Oxford, where he entered himself as a servitor at Exeter College.[8]

This sent him into a feverish frenzy of asking friends and family to help him financially. He even began publishing booklets of some of the poems that he had written in the hope that the funds would help him pay off his debts.

In spite of his poverty and indebtedness, he did not stop helping others in need. His first year at Oxford was one of the coldest recorded and, again from Dallimore's account:

> As he was walking one morning, he came upon a small boy, very poorly clad, lying beneath a hedge and crying from hunger and cold. Samuel had in his pocket two pennies—all that he owned—but he was so moved by the little lad's suffering that he gave him both of them. The boy ran to buy bread for himself and his still younger sister. But a very welcome surprise greeted the now penniless Samuel when he returned to his college. He found that a relative had

sent him five shillings and that a gift from his mother was waiting for him. She had sent him a cheese.[9]

As his years of schooling went on, Samuel managed to support himself, although at one time he came to a very low point where he decided that he would have to leave Oxford altogether. He even wrote a poem about his departure, "but when returning a book he had borrowed he accidentally left this poem in it. The owner of the book, a senior student, found these farewell verses and was so moved by them that he took steps to see that Wesley would not need to leave the University."[10] The book's owner paid his debts and arranged for Samuel to be a tutor for struggling students, and also ensured that they paid him well for his services.

In June of 1688 he graduated from Oxford, and returned to London where he was ordained as a minister of the Church of England, which ensured that he would be paid a yearly wage. Now he could support the girl he wanted to marry, nineteen-year-old Susanna Annesley, whom he had known for approximately six years. They were married on November 11, 1688.

Susanna Annesley Wesley
(1669-1742)

EARLY MARRIED LIFE FOR SUSANNA

Married life for Susanna and Samuel was not a walk in the park. His ministry provided only a small amount of money to live on each year. Susanna became pregnant very quickly and, because of their financial difficulties, she went to live with her parents. (She and her father must have maintained a good relationship even though he had not been invited to her Church of England wedding ceremony.)

"On 10 February 1690, in the home in which she had spent her girlhood, she gave birth to a son, who, like his father and grandfather, was given the name of Samuel."[11]A letter that she wrote to her first son much later in his life proves that she suffered a difficult labor with him: "You, my son—you who was once the son of my extremist sorrow in your birth. . . ."[12]

By this time her husband Samuel had been bouncing from one position to another. He took on a new position as a curate (a clergyman who assists a vicar), but he could not afford to focus solely on that job. He tried to combine his duties with a literary job in London, but this did not sit well with his superiors and they soon let him go. During this time the small family was living in a boarding house. When Samuel was offered a new position as a rector (pastor) of Saint Leonard's Church in South Ormsby, Lincolnshire, the distance between their living quarters and the church entailed transportation costs for himself, his wife, and new son, which only added more debt.

Debt seemed to be a pattern for Samuel throughout his life. Samuel's debt increased still further when he moved to South Ormsby, because he possessed no furniture. Having to buy some, he had hoped that Dr. Annesley would provide the money, but he did not. Apparently, the Dissenting doctor was not ready to assist his Anglican son-in-law by furnishing his house for him.

He began his pastorate in the month of June, 1690. South

Ormsby was very small village of only about 260 people. Life for the young bride must have been most difficult, but she seemed to accommodate herself to her circumstances. Later in life, she said, "I am content to fill a little space if God be glorified."[13] Dallimore writes:

> We do well to remind ourselves that such a house, in a country village, was completely lacking in the host of conveniences that are found in almost all of our houses today. There was no electricity for lighting or heating and none of domestic appliances that operate on it, no refrigerator, radio or television, no telephone or running water. There were fires to light and water had to be drawn from a well or carried from a stream. Because everything had to be done by hand, all but the poorest homes would employ a girl as a servant, and such help could be obtained for about four pence a day. The Wesleys kept one servant most of the time and on occasions when Susanna was incapacitated they had two. This was not a special privilege, but was the practice in a large number of homes, and would have been expected in a clergyman's household.[14]

Susanna and Samuel lived in South Ormsby for a while where he worked and also helped his brother-in-law

> I can do all things through Christ which strengtheneth me. (Philippians 4:13)

John Dunton in a bi-weekly journal where he would answer Bible questions such as, "On what day did Adam fall?" "How do angels eat?" "How shall infants and deformed persons rise at the Day of Judgment?" and "Whither went the waters of Noah's flood?"[15] During this time of living in South Ormsby he wrote two books, one entitled *An Essay Upon All Sorts of Learning* and *A Discourse Concerning the Antiquity and Authority of Hebrew Vowel Points*. (Surely *Hebrew Vowel Points* was a hot seller!) Clearly, Samuel was well-schooled, and he possessed a considerable amount of knowledge for a man of his time. Clearly also, Susanna had to sacrifice much for him because of his dedicated hours of study. He seemed to take 2 Timothy 2:15 to mean that he should devote himself to such pursuits ("Be diligent to present yourself approved to God as a workman who does not need to be ashamed, accurately handling the word of truth").

Samuel wrote some of his thoughts toward his wife during this season of their life together. He explained how she was a blessing to him, and yet one can detect some conviction on his part for treating her harshly, especially by his words, "I bore an undisputed sway." In other words, he may have been like a taskmaster, while she was quick to serve and obey him. Here is Samuel's poem about Susanna:

> She graced my humble roof, and blest my life,
> Blest me by a far greater name than wife;
> Yet still I bore an undisputed sway,
> Nor was't her task, but pleasure to obey:
> Scarce thought, much less could act, what I denied.
> In our low house there was no room for pride;
> Nor need I e'er direct what still was right,
> She studied my convenience day and night,
> Nor did I for her care ungrateful prove,
> But only used my power to show my love;
> Whate'er she asked I gave without reproach or grudge,

For still she reason asked, and I was judge.[16]

One can only imagine how difficult it was to submit to a man as demanding as Samuel, especially since Susanna had a very independent spirit (as demonstrated by her decision to leave the dissenting group that her father was part of). Arnold Dallimore in his book, *"Susanna Wesley"* wrote:

Married life was not proving a great success from Susanna's point of view. Not only was she not allowed a mind of her own, they were also living in poverty and her husband was constantly in debt. She had grown up in her father's comfortable home, but since marrying Samuel Wesley she had lived, first in the boarding-house, and now in this primitive rectory at South Ormsby. Similarly, her father had never known financial need, but it was becoming obvious that Samuel would probably remain in debt for the rest of his days. So by the time she had been married a few months, Susanna must have come to realize that submission and poverty were likely to be permanent features of her life.[17]

By this time a second child was born, also named "Susanna." And one year later another daughter named Emilia came along. Susanna suffered from regular bouts of rheumatism, which forced her to stay off her feet. This caused Samuel to remark: ". . . my wife's lying about last Christmas and threatening to do the same the next, and two children and as many servants to provide for (my wife being sickly, having had three or four touches of her rheumatism again, though we always fight it away with whey). . . ."[18]

Their first child, Sammy, worried them. Even at four years of age he was not yet talking. Then one day out of the blue, he began speaking in clear sentences, and he was fine from that day forward.

In the year 1694, they experienced the first tragic death within their family, and it certainly would not be the last. Their first daughter and second child, Susanna, passed away after being sick for months. One year later, Susanna gave birth to twin boys who only lived for one month.

Then in 1696, Susanna had to say good-bye to her father Samuel, who had fallen ill. Susanna had been very close to her father and as a result she took his death very hard, although he himself seemed to be ready for death. At the very end of his life he had said:

> Blessed be God. I have been faithful in the work of the ministry above fifty-five years! I have no doubt, nor shadow of doubt! All is clear between God and my soul. He chains up Satan; he cannot trouble me.

Precious in the sight of the Lord is the death of His saints. (Psalm 116:15)
Jesus said unto her, I am the resurrection, and the life: he that believeth in me, though he were dead, yet shall he live. (John 11:25)
Now if we be dead with Christ, we believe that we shall also live with him: Knowing that Christ being raised from the dead dieth no more; death hath no more dominion over him. For in that he died, he died unto sin once: but in that he liveth, he liveth unto God. (Romans 6:8–10)
The Lord killeth, and maketh alive: he bringeth down to the grave, and bringeth up. (1 Samuel 2:6)

Come, dear Jesus! The nearer the more precious,

and the more welcome. . . .

I cannot contain it! What manner of love is this to a poor worm! I cannot express a thousandth part of what praise is due to Thee! We know not what we do when we aim at praising God for His mercies! It is but little I can give; but, Lord, help me to give Thee my all! I will die praising Thee, and rejoice that there are others that can praise Thee better. I shall be satisfied with Thy likeness!—Satisfied!—Satisfied!—O, my dearest Jesus, I come![19]

Susanna had difficulty coming to terms with the fact that her father had actually left this earth. Historians tell us that "Her son John heard her say that she was frequently as fully persuaded that her father was with her, as if she had seen him with her bodily eyes."[20]

At the end of seven long years of living in South Ormsby, Susanna and Samuel prepared to leave, hoping for the grass to be "greener on the other side" at Epworth, where Samuel would be the rector for the next thirty-eight years. Their whole time in South Ormsby had been difficult. Susanna had been in constant pregnancy, struggling with health and debt. The good news was that Samuel's yearly salary would go from £50 to £200, but as everyone knows, money does not buy happiness. Susanna and her Prince Charming's struggles were nowhere near over.

CHAPTER 4

SUSANNA'S VIEWS ON RAISING GODLY CHILDREN

W E CAN GLEAN many insights from Susanna Wesley's life, but perhaps one of the most valuable ones is how to raise godly children. Her approach can be summed up in a few words; she is quoted as having said:

> The parent who studies to subdue self-will in his child works together with God in the saving of a soul. The parent who indulges self-will does the devil's work, makes religion impractical, salvation unattainable and does all that is in him to drown his child, soul and body forever.[1]

SONS AND DAUGHTERS

Between 1690 and 1709, Susanna Wesley gave birth to nineteen children, including three sets of twins. We know the names of fourteen of the children, and a little bit about their lives (needless to say, we know a great deal more about her famous sons Charles and John Wesley than we do about the others):

Samuel was her oldest child, and was born in either the year 1690 or 1691; scholars have not been able to determine the exact year. (Once he wrote a letter that he was born in 1690, but his tombstone says he died in his forty-ninth year, which would put his birth in 1691.[2] As an adult,

Samuel was a gifted poet, teacher, organist, hymn writer, and clergyman. He obtained a Master's degree from Oxford University. He disapproved of the Methodist movement, but he supported his brothers in their efforts. He was such a generous son that he provided his parents with all of his salary. His mother was heartbroken when he died in 1739, as he was her chief source of support.

Emilia ("Emily") was born in January of 1692, making her the oldest daughter. She lived a long life and died in London at the age of seventy-nine. Late in life, at the age of forty-four, she married Robert Harper, an apothecary, and had one child who died of illness. Her brother John officiated at her wedding. At one point her husband left her, taking all of their savings. She had a good ear for music and poetry, was a governess until she felt the need to go back home and take care of her ill family. Eventually, she became a Methodist, following the steps of her brothers John and Charles.

Twin sons named Annesley (after Susanna's maiden name) and Jedediah were born in 1694 but died the following year.[3]

Susanna ("Sukey") was born in South Ormsby in 1695. As a young woman, she married a wealthy farmer, and had four children with him, and in 1731 almost died giving birth. Her husband treated her so poorly that after a fire destroyed their home she fled with the children to London. He went to great lengths to find her, going so far as to announce his own death in the newspaper, but was unsuccessful. She died at age sixty-nine, in London.

Mary ("Molly") was born a cripple in 1696, also in South

Ormsby. Many family members never expected her to marry due to her disability, but she fell in love with a member of the clergy, John Whitelamb, her father's curate. Sadly, she died after only one year of marriage, at age thirty-eight, during childbirth.

Mehetabel ("Hetty") was born at Epworth in 1697 and lived until age fifty-three. She showed great intellectual promise; by the age of only eight, she could read the Gospel of Mark in Greek. But as a young woman, she fell in love with a young lawyer of whom her father did not approve. They decided to elope, but after one night together did not go through with the marriage. She came home pregnant, married an illiterate plumber in haste, and gave birth to a daughter. Her father withheld his forgiveness from her and never spoke to her again. Her marriage to the plumber was not a good one, and she lost all of her subsequent children to early deaths.

Some sources say that Susanna's next children were stillborn twins. Then a baby boy named John was born in 1699, and he died as an infant. And another son named Benjamin, who was born in 1700, also died while yet a babe in arms. Yet another child (unnamed) was born and died the following year, in 1701.

Anne ("Nancy") was born in Epworth in 1702 as a twin. Her twin brother died seven months after their birth. She was happily married to a land surveyor name John Lambert, a well-educated man.

John Wesley was born in 1703 and lived to the ripe old age of eighty-seven. A rectory fire which occurred on

February 9, 1709, when Wesley was five years old, left an indelible impression. Here is the often-told story from his childhood:

> Some time after 11:00 p.m., the rectory roof caught on fire. Sparks falling on the children's beds and cries of "fire" from the street roused the Wesleys who managed to shepherd all their children out of the house except for John who was left stranded on the second floor. With stairs aflame and the roof about to collapse, Wesley was lifted out of the second floor window by a parishioner standing on another man's shoulders. Wesley later utilized the phrase, "a brand plucked out of the fire," quoting Zechariah 3:2, to describe the incident. This childhood deliverance subsequently became part of the Wesley legend, attesting to his special destiny and extraordinary work."[4]

John became a prominent theologian and evangelist who frequently preached in the open air. He was the founder of Methodism and was close friends of George Whitfield. He married his only wife, Mary Vazeille, at age forty-four, but never had children by her. She was a wealthy widow and came into the marriage with four children. For several years she joined John on his speaking engagements; however, she was a jealous wife and their marriage was a struggle. Twenty years into their marriage she left him.

Martha was born in Epworth in 1706. She lived the longest of all the sisters, dying at age eighty-five. Because of her long life she was able to communicate important information about her family's life to a biographer named

Adam Clarke, the first biographer of the Wesley family. She married Wesley Hall, a member of the Holy Club, who apparently wasn't so holy after all, because he was unfaithful. She left him.

Charles Wesley, younger brother to John and the eighteenth child, was born in 1707 and died in 1788 at age eighty-one. When he was born prematurely, his survival was uncertain. He is remembered to this day for the thousands of hymns that he wrote, one of the most famous of which is "Hark the Herald Angels Sing."

Kezia was born in 1709. Susanna was forty when she gave birth to Kezia. Kezia never married and did not have good health, dying at age thirty-two. Once when Wesley Hall came to visit the family, he "forgot" that he was married to Martha and tried to romance her sister Kezia. She was brokenhearted over the false profession of love Hall made to her.

> Jonathan Edwards said, "Every Christian family ought to be as it were a little church, consecrated to Christ, and wholly influenced and governed by his rules. And family education and order are some of the chief means of grace."

The Puritans believed that the home was the primary place of learning the Bible and moral instruction. They also believed that it was a parent's spiritual responsibility to disciple and teach their children about faith. Susanna strongly followed this line of

> George Whitefield, one of John Wesley's best friends, said, "A man ought to look upon himself as obliged to act in three capacities: as a prophet, to instruct; as a priest, to pray for and with; as a king, to govern, direct, and provide for them." [his children]

thinking as she took care of her very large family.

If you want "godly offspring," it is essential that you make the time to establish a family altar. Build it out of the unmovable rocks of resolution. You will need to be resolute about this because it will be a battle. Your flesh will fight it, and you can be sure there will be a continual spiritual battle within your mind. "Circumstances" will constantly crop up. Your kids will occasionally groan when you announce that it is time for devotions. Loved ones may subtly, subconsciously, discourage you. However, your time of family devotions should be a priority for your whole family. Don't be legalistic about it, but as much as possible, put all other things aside before you postpone or cancel family devotions.

It will be an altar of sacrifice, as you sacrifice your time, your energy, and sometimes your dignity. For years, our kids heard, "Six o'clock—reading time." My wife and I dropped whatever we were doing, and the children learned to do the same, and we gathered as a family. Making it a priority, for your family's growth will speak volumes about its importance in their lives. You will find that there are many excuses for not having devotions. You may be pressed for time, feel tired, or think you are unable to teach the Bible. However, there is one very powerful reason why you should have daily devotions: the eternal salvation of your children.

—Ray Comfort

The Bible instructs us, "Train up a child in the way he should go: and when he is old he will not depart from it" (Proverbs 22:6). It is important for children to begin learning about God and the Bible at home and Susanna took this task to heart.

SUSANNA'S RULES

Susannah Wesley spent one hour each day praying for her children. In addition, she took each child aside for a full hour every week to discuss spiritual matters with him or her. No wonder two of her sons, Charles and John, were used of God to bring blessing to all of England and much of America.

Here are a few rules she followed in training her children:

1. Subdue self-will in a child and thus work together with God to save his soul.

2. Teach him to pray as soon as he can speak.

3. Give him nothing he cries for and only what is good for him if he asks for it politely.

4. To prevent lying, punish no fault which is freely confessed, but never allow a rebellious, sinful act to go unnoticed.

5. Commend and reward good behavior.

6. Strictly observe all promises you have made to your child.[5]

SUSANNA'S SCHOOLHOUSE

Susanna and Samuel's marriage proved to be a rocky one. He was absent a lot, and had to work often because of his continual debts. On one occasion, he and Susanna were praying together and she would not say amen to his prayer for the king. So, he left her alone with the children for approximately one year. Finally, he returned home but their relationship was strained. Susanna began to turn inward and focus almost solely on her children and the duties at home. History tells us that she said in regards to these things, "I have lived such a retired life for so many years. . . . No one can, without renouncing the world in the most literal sense, observe my method; and there are few, if any, that would entirely devote above twenty years of the prime of life in hopes to save the souls of their children."[6]

After losing several children in infancy, Susanna had Anne and John. Then she lost another infant in a tragic accident when the child was suffocated by the nurse.[7] Even though she faced many losses, she pressed on and poured her entire soul into the ten remaining children who would later become influential in society; their influence can be attributed to Susanna's education and oversight.

What did Susanna do to pour into the lives of her children? We can only imagine that this was an escape for her as well from her troubles with Samuel. We can safely assume that the more she attended her children, the less she thought about the trials and her dysfunction relationship with her husband. She set up a school in her home where she could efficiently teach the children daily. Even after a fire destroyed everything, she still found a way to make a schoolroom for the children. Classes were conducted six days a week, from 9:00 A.M. to 12:00 noon and from 2:00 P.M. to 5:00 P.M. "There was no such thing as loud talking or playing allowed", stated Susanna, "but everyone was kept close to business for the six hours of school."[8]

This type of school schedule is unheard-of today. We have come a long way from this type of schedule and would do well to learn from Susanna's order and discipline. Proverbs 12:1 says, "Whoso loveth instruction loveth knowledge: but he that hateth reproof is brutish." This would have been a perfect verse for Susanna to have on her wall at home.

Susanna was very consistent in disciplining her children from their earliest stages of life. As she explained it:

> The children were always put into a regular method of living, in such things as they were capable of, from their birth; as in dressing and undressing, changing their linen, etc. . . . When they turned a year old (and some before) they were taught to fear the rod and to cry softly, by which means they escaped abundance of correction . . . and that most odious noise of the crying of children was rarely heard in the house.[9]

Arnold Dallimore, in his book on Susanna Wesley's life, assures us that her discipline was light when compared to what was happening in other schools. He says, "In schools, beating with the birch rod was considered as necessary

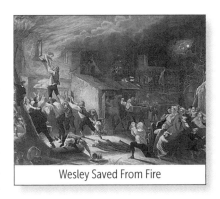

Wesley Saved From Fire

as teaching the alphabet and many parents assumed that physical punishment of their children was as essential for them as eating. In contrast with such conditions, Susanna's discipline was light and constructive." Susanna must have read Proverbs 29:15 which says, "The rod and reproof give wisdom: but a child left to himself bringeth his mother to shame." Biographer Kirk wrote:

> No sooner were her children born into the world, than their infant life was regulated by method. Even their sleep was meted out in strict accordance with

rule. The appointed time for their slumber—three hours in the morning and three in the afternoon—was gradually shortened, until they required none at all during the day time. Punctual till the moment they were laid in the cradle, awake if possible, and rocked to sleep. The gentle motion was continued until the allotted time had transpired, and then, awake or asleep, they were taken up. This method secured their daily rest and regulated the time of its duration. The common apology for the peevishness of a child as the evening approaches was never heard in the Wesley family. At 7:00, immediately after supper, they were all prepared for bed; and at 8:00 they were left in their several rooms awake; "for there was no such thing allowed in the house as sitting by a child until it went to sleep."[10]

Not only did Susanna regulate the children's school habits and bedtime, but she also disciplined with how much they ate. As soon as they grew up a bit they only were allowed three meals a day. They were not allowed to eat and snack in between meals. Any of her children who might venture outside of this parameter would have been severely beaten. At each meal they had family prayers, and "at these meals they were never allowed to eat of more than one thing, and of that sparingly enough."[11] The children were not allowed to ask for anything they wanted, and their little table and chairs were positioned so that Susanna and any of the servants were able to look after them. "They whispered their want to the servant who attended them, and she conveyed their request to the mother."[12] They soon learned to eat and drink what was set before them.

This discipline paid off; the children learned how to buffet their bodies and not give in to fleshly lusts. Proof of this is that when any of the children fell sick, they had no trouble in taking medicine that was bitter. The children learned to cry very softly so that every neighbor on the block would not hear them. About her approach to childrearing, Susanna wrote:

In order to firm the minds of children, the first thing to be done is to conquer their will and bring them to an obedient temper. To inform the understanding is a work of time, and must with children proceed by small degrees as they are able to bear it; but the subjecting the will is a thing that must be done at one, and the sooner the better, for by neglecting timely correction they will contract stubbornness and obstinacy which are hardly ever after painful to me as to the child. . . . And when the will of a child is totally subdued, and it is brought to revere and stand in awe of the parents, then a great many childish follies and inadvertencies may be passed by. Some should be overlooked and taken no notice of, and others mildly reproved; but no willful transgression ought ever to be forgiven children

> If you've ever seen the television show "The Dog Whisperer" you know what it looks like for dog trainer Cesar Millan to make the dog be calm and submissive. Maybe you've seen an episode where he has to pin the dog on the ground on its side to make it surrender its will. When you first see him doing this maneuver you feel pity for the dog, but soon begin to understand what he is doing is necessary to break the dog's will and to show him who the pack leader is.

without chastisement, less or more, as the nature and circumstances of the offence may require.[13]

Susanna's breaking of her children's wills was a way of getting them to see who was in charge. Under this type of instruction and discipline her children flourished and progressed very rapidly. Susanna wrote, "It is almost incredible what a child may be taught in a quarter of a year by a vigorous application. . . . All could read better in that time than most women can do as long as they live."

Michelle Duggar on Teaching Self Control to Children

Like Susanna Wesley, Michelle Duggar has nineteen children. We could call her a modern-day "Susanna." Listen to her insightful words on child rearing taken from the family blog:

To instill self-control in her children—especially her energetic little boys—Michelle uses a process that she calls Quiet and Still. From the time they are young, the mother of many teaches her kids to sit quietly, and slowly increases the length of time. "It's not waiting until they do something wrong to correct them, but actually taking moments to train them," explains Michelle.

She recommends starting with increments of five minutes. Here's how it works: "I'll sit him in a chair, and I'll say, 'Okay, Mommy's going to sit beside you, and you're going to practice being still and quiet . . . yes ma'am?'. . . We may do that two or three times a day for about a week, and usually they catch it. What they're learning is self-control. They're learning to obey Mommy's voice."

One of Michelle's favorite mantras is, "The first time I say it, you obey it." "Then it can be transferred to when you're in the grocery store and they're sitting in the cart. . . . They can learn to do that wherever they are, because it's trained into their little hearts."

Michelle also stresses the importance of pouring out the praise. She and Jim Bob believe that one of the most vital parenting tips is to "praise your children ten times more than you correct them."

Arnold Dallimore, in his book on Susanna's life, talks about the importance of the Bible being at the center of all things. He goes on to explain that "class is opened each morning with the singing of a psalm and the reading of the scriptures and they closed with the same exercise. The children were trained, as in all venues of their lives in decency and politeness."[14] What this meant, according to Susanna, is that "taking God's name in vain, cursing and swearing, profanity, obscenity, rude ill-bred names were never heard among them."[15]

More of Susanna's House Rules

1. Eating between meals not allowed.
2. As children they are to be in bed by 8:00 p.m.
3. They are required to take medicine without complaining.
4. Subdue self-will in a child, and those working together with God to save the child's soul.
5. To teach a child to pray as soon as he can speak.
6. Require all to be still during Family Worship.
7. Give them nothing that they cry for, and only that when asked for politely.
8. To prevent lying, punish no fault which is first confessed and repented of.
9. Never allow a sinful act to go unpunished.
10. Never punish a child twice for a single offense.
11. Comment and reward good behavior.
12. Any attempt to please, even if poorly performed, should be commended.
13. Preserve property rights, even in smallest matters.
14. Strictly observe all promises.
15. Require no daughter to work before she can read well.
16. Teach children to fear the rod.[17]

SUSANNA'S DEFINITION OF "SIN"

As a young man, John Wesley asked his mother for a definition of sin. She replied in a letter:

> Whatever weakens your reason, impairs the tenderness of your conscience, obscures your sense of God, takes off your relish for spiritual things, whatever increases the authority of the body over the mind, that thing is sin to you, however innocent it may seem in itself.[16]

Susanna was an extraordinary woman, and her children clearly looked up to her. A lot of that comes from her consistency and discipline with them. They knew what she expected of them, and they, in return, had assurances from her. Her House Rules were implemented to instill a sense of self-control over sin, and ultimately obedience to God.

SUSANNA ON DISCIPLINE

Susannah Wesley believed that for a child to grow into a *self-disciplined* adult, he or she must first be a *parent-disciplined* child. To her, the stubborn flesh was the hardest battle for Christians to fight, and godly parents would do well to equip their children to overcome it early.[18]

She wrote:

> When the will of a child is totally subdued, and it is brought to revere and stand in awe of the parents, then a great many childish follies may be passed by. I insist on the conquering of the will of children betimes, because this is the only strong and

rational foundation of a religious education when this is thoroughly done, then a child is capable of being governed by reason and piety.[19]

A Word for Moms

I know well that a mother's tasks in the home, caring for her children, are not light. It is no easy thing to go on in the same routine, day after day, week after week, month after month . . . always keeping sweet, always having a shining face and a cheerful word, always strong to meet every question and perplexity and difficulty which comes to you. But I want to say a word of encouragement to you. The mother's place is the highest place to which any woman can be called! When God puts into your hand a little child . . . to care for, to guide, to teach, to watch over, to inspire and train for life and eternity—He puts upon you serious responsibility. But He also promises the strength you need, and the help for every experience. One of Augustine's great prayers was, "Command what You will—and then give what You command." That is the way God always does, if we trust Him and go forward in simple confidence. Whatever He commands us to do—He will help us to do. Nothing is impossible when we have Christ with us and in us. I want to help you to enter upon your days, whatever their care may be, with the confidence that your Master is with you and is going to help you to get through everything beautifully, victoriously and sweetly. It is a great thing to be able to live victoriously, amid all the cares and frets and frictions and trials of everyday life.

—J.R. Miller, *Intimate Letters on Personal Problems,* 1914

William Nicholson in his 1862 sermon called "Divine Comfort!" had insightful words on God our great comforter:

As a mother comforts her child—so will I comfort you; and you shall be comforted." Isaiah 66:13

The condescending love of God to sinners is most astonishing. Though He is the High and Lofty One—yet He knows, pities, and cares for worms of the earth—sinful, frail, dying men. Human language is insufficient to express the heights and depths of Divine compassion.

God is called, "The Father of compassion and the God of all comfort, who comforts us in all our troubles" (2 Corinthians 1:3-4). Also, "God, who comforts the downcast" (2 Corinthians 7:6).

God's divine comfort is most endearing and effective. "As a mother comforts her child—so will I comfort you." This is a beautiful and striking comparison. No other relationship can so expressively represent the parental kindness of God, as an affectionate mother caring for her beloved child.

1. God will comfort His people with all the affection and solicitude of a mother. See the mother—how she loves, strives, labors, suffers, and sacrifices for her child.

   A mother watches over and defends her child. So does our heavenly Father. He is a wall of fire, a refuge, a strong tower, a shield, a rock of strength, a fortress, a very present help in times of trouble, etc., etc.

   A mother is solicitous to care and provide for her child. "And my God will meet all your needs according to His glorious riches in Christ Jesus!" "Casting all your care on Him, because He cares about you!"

2. God will comfort His people with all the patience and forbearance of a mother. "For He Himself knows our frame; He is mindful that we are but dust!" (Psalm 103:14). "The Lord is compassionate and gracious, slow to anger and abounding in lovingkindness!" (Psalm 103:8).

3. God will comfort His people with all the forgiveness and consolation of a mother. How ready is she to forgive her erring, wandering child— and how ready to console in trouble! "The Lord has comforted His people and will have compassion on His afflicted" (Isaiah 49:13).

4. God will comfort His people with all the instruction and correction of a mother. A good and wise mother will both instruct and correct. Just so, "the Lord disciplines the one He loves, and chastises every son whom He receives" (Hebrews 12:6).

5. God will comfort His people with all the constancy of a mother. When does the love of a mother end? "Can a woman forget her nursing child, that she should have no compassion on the son of her womb? Even these may forget—yet I will not forget you. Behold, I have engraved you on the palms of my hands!" (Isaiah 49:15-16). "Having loved His own who were in the world, He loved them to the end!" (John 13:1).20

Outside view of the Epworth Old Rectory

Rectory Gardens

Charles Wesley's music stand

Susanna Wesley's kitchen

The path from the village leading to St. Andrew's Parish Church

Interior - looking toward the sanctuary

Interior - looking toward the nave[21]

CHAPTER 5

SUSANNA'S TRIUMPHS AND TRIALS

It is certainly true that I have had a large experience of what the world calls adverse fortune.

—Susanna Wesley[1]

SUSANNA WESLEY'S LIFE was full of both trials and tribulations. She experienced sickness and the death of nine children. One of her daughters had a pregnancy out of wedlock. She endured Samuel's many imprisonments, perpetual money problems, and the sorrow of being a widow. Because she and her husband, Samuel, worked so hard to shape their children in deep Christian learning and devotion, you would think that each of their children would grow up to marry well and establish their own devout Christian families, yet it did not work out that way.

Of the seven bright daughters of Samuel and Susanna, five had marriages that were unsatisfactory, and at least two were disastrous, one of those being Hetty's. We can learn from historical accounts that Hetty, without much thought, ran off with a man, and, after being away for some time, returned home pregnant. When her father found out about her condition, he was enraged and irreconcilable. Hetty, out of both contrition and desperation, volunteered to marry any man her parents chose, in an attempt to cover, or at least in some way to redeem, her indiscretion.

It was said that, "Her father unwisely approved her union with a drunken and illiterate plumber, a Mr. Wright, though her father would not marry them. Four months later the child was born but did not survive. Her other children also did not live. Her life was an ever-deepening tragedy."[2] Other circumstances contributed to the disappointing outcome of her family life: grinding poverty, a deprived social environment, a scarcity of eligible mates for refined young women, and having a father who was considered a serious and competent rector of the church but who seemed to lack wisdom for the regulation of his home and family.[3]

SUSANNA ABANDONED BY SAMUEL

Samuel had hopes of moving to a better home, as he and Susanna made an advancement to South Ormsby to Epworth. His hopes included ministry and preaching in this new city. During this time, he was invited to London where he would speak in front of various audiences. One particular meeting where he spoke was for was the Society For The Reformation Of Manners. There were not only ministers there but people of great influence and wealth. But as you can imagine traveling was very expensive and Samuel had to foot the bill, putting them further into debt. By 1700 Samuel was in so much debt that he became desperate, so he wrote to the Archbishop of York where he pleaded his financial burdens and asked for pardon. The Archbishop had mercy on him. In spite of this pardon, his debts were still insurmountable, and it seems that he possibly took it out on Susanna.

John Wesley wrote about this time in his parent's marriage, which had happened before he was born, but had been recounted to him:

The year before King William died my father observed my mother did not say "Amen" to the prayer for the king. She said she could not, for she did not believe that the Prince of Orange was king. He vowed he would not cohabit with her till she did. He then took horse and rode away, nor did she hear anything of him for a twelvemonth. He then came back and lived with her as before. But I fear his vow was not forgotten before God.[4]

Dallimore adds more about this time when she would not say amen to Samuel's prayer. He writes:

Various authors, seeking to maintain that Samuel's character was entirely unblemished, have declared that this "Amen" affair never happened. They have asserted that John got hold of a false tale and assumed it to be true. The Rev. Luke Tyerman, for instance, says, "The one damaging point, that Samuel Wesley allowed a miserable squabble respecting the rights of King William to make him neglect his wife, and to leave his house, his family and his flock for the space of twelve months, is a thing which, if true, would have been a scandalous, cruel and wicked act."[5]

Sadly, it does appear that John Wesley was not mistaken. His father did indeed abandon his mother for an entire year. Several letters dating from 1701–1702 give proof. During this time of abandonment, their house caught on fire. (This was a different fire from the one from which John was rescued.) The danger was very great. On hearing of the fire, Samuel borrowed a horse and hurried home, where he learned, he wrote, "that my wife, children and books were saved."[6]

LOSS OF NINE CHILDREN

Early in May, 1705, Mrs. Wesley gave birth to another son, but between "worry and weakness was unable to nurse it, so it was given into the charge of a woman who lived opposite the rectory."[7] Apparently, because of a contested election, the Epworth street was so noisy one night with people shouting and firing pistols that the nurse could not get to "sleep till between one and two in the morning, and then slept so soundly that she overlaid and killed the child."[8]

Here is the father's account of what happened. Samuel wrote:

> I went to Lincoln on Tuesday night, May 29th, and the Election began on Wednesday, 30th. A great part of the night our Isle people kept drumming, shouting, and firing of pistols and guns under the window where my wife lay, who had been brought to bed not three weeks. I had put the child to nurse over against my own house: the noise kept his nurse waking till one or two in the morning. Then they left off, and the nurse, being heavy to sleep, overlaid the child. She waked and finding it dead, ran over with it to my house, almost distracted, and calling my servants, threw it into their arms. They, as wise as she, ran up with it to my wife, and before she was well awake, threw it cold and dead into hers. She composed herself as well as she could, and that day got it buried.[9]

John Kirk gives further insight into this tragic event:

> Sadly, this child's death was one of nine children

who died very young. It is difficult to determine how many of their nineteen children were living at one time. Only seven daughters and three sons grew up to maturity. But John Wesley speaks with profound admiration of the serenity with which his Mother wrote letters, attended to business, and held conversations while surrounded by thirteen children. More than ten, therefore, must have survived the period of infancy though the nine departed ones evidently died young. The first breach in the domestic circle—an event never to be forgotten wherever it occurs—was made in the spring of 1693, when Susanna, the second child and first daughter, only two years old, was summoned away. The following year the grace again closed; this time over the twin brothers, Annesley and Jedediah, children of a few weeks. Then at intervals, probably too short to allow the wounded heart to heal, others fell by the hand of the destroyer, until the trial culminated with the infant accidentally suffocated by the nurse. These repeated bereavements were borne with becoming resignation to the Divine will; but they, nevertheless, deeply wrung the Mother's heart. One sentence, penned many years after they had taken place, discloses the feeling with which she remembered her losses, "I have buried many but here I must pause!" Poor sorrowing Mother, weeping over the graves of the early dead,

"Think what a present thou to God hast sent,

And render Him with patience what He lent:

This if thou do, He will an offspring give,

That till the world's last end shall make thy name to live!"

Mrs. Wesley's care for those who died in childhood was soon over; but the ten survivors claimed her untiring attention and industry for many years.[10]

SAMUEL ARRESTED

If it wasn't enough for Susanna to lose a baby, another unexpected trial was around the corner; Samuel was arrested eighteen days after the baby's death. The effects these trials had on Susanna and the children are best told by Samuel himself. Not surprisingly, he was in debt to an individual he had upset by his passion and zeal at the recent election, and, because he did not pay he was arrested and sent to Lincoln jail. Here is the account written by his own pen to the Archbishop of York:

Lincoln Castle, June 25th, 1705

Now I am at rest, for I am come to the haven where I've long expected to be. On Friday last (June 23rd), when I had been, in christening a child, at Epworth, I was arrested in my churchyard by one who had been my servant, and gathered my tithe last year, at the suit of one of Mr. Whichcott's relations and zealous friends (Mr. Pinder), according to their promise when they were in the Isle before the Election. The sum was not thirty pounds, but it was as good as five hundred. Now they knew the burning of my flax, my London journey, and their throwing me out of my regiment, had both sunk my credit and exhausted my money. My adversary was sent to where I was on the road, to meet me, that I might make some proposals to him. But all his answer (which I have by me) was, that I must immediately pay the whole sum or go to prison. Thither I went with no great concern for myself, and find much more civility and satisfaction here than in *bevibus gyaris* of my own Epworth. I thank God, my wife was pretty well recovered, and churched some days before I was taken from her; and hope she'll be able to look to my family, if they don't turn them out of doors, as they have often threatened to do. One of my biggest concerns was my being forced to leave my poor lambs in the midst of so many wolves. But the great Shepherd is able to provide for them, and to preserve them. My wife bears it with that courage which becomes her, and which I expected from her. I don't despair of doing some good here (and so long I shan't lose quite the end of living), and, it may be, do more in this parish than in my old one; for I have leave to read prayers every morning and afternoon here in the prison, and to preach once a Sunday, which I choose to do in the afternoon when there is no sermon at the minster. And I'm getting acquainted with my brother jail-birds as fast as I can; and shall write to London, next post, to the Society for Propagating Christian Knowledge, who, I hope, will send me some books to distribute amongst them. I should not write these things from a jail if I thought your Grace would believe me ever the less for my being here; where if I should lay my bones, I 'd bless God and pray for your Grace. Your Grace's very obliged and most humble servant, S. WESLEY.[11]

Susanna was heroic during her husband's imprisonment. After his imprisonment, she was subject to a myriad of insults and threats. She and the children and everybody in the parsonage were living in a constant state of struggle and apprehension. Yet Susanna carried on bravely. Samuel wrote about her:

> 'Tis not every one could bear these things; but, I bless God, my wife is less concerned with suffering them, than I am in the writing. She is not dependent upon the produce of the dairy for the subsistence of the family, and absolutely destitute of money, her anxieties would certainly have crushed a woman of inferior spirit, and less confidence in the God of her life. She felt deeply lest her husband should be in greater straits for necessary food than herself and children. What little jewelry she possessed, including "the token and pledge" of her marriage covenant, she send for his relief. It was instantly returned, "and God soon provided for him."[12]

God often uses suffering to draw us near to himself. During difficult times, He is sanctifying and shaping us into the image of his Son. We cannot think that we will have glory without the cross or that we will escape suffering in this present evil age.

God uses chronic pain and weakness, along with other afflictions, as His chisel for sculpting our lives. Felt weakness deepens dependence on Christ for strength each day. The weaker we feel, the harder we lean. And the harder we lean, the stronger we grow spiritually, even while our bodies waste away. To live with your "thorn" uncomplainingly—that is, sweet, patient, and free in heart to love and help others, even though every day you feel weak—is true sanctification. It is true healing for the spirit. It is a supreme victory of grace.[13]

—J.I. Packer

MONEY PROBLEMS

Money in the Wesley house was scarce, and Samuel was put into debtor's prison more than once, leaving Susanna to figure out how to provide on her own. Despite this, she was a dedicated wife who expressed her affection for her husband in the highest terms, ever willing to stand by him and vindicate his honor. Even when he was criticized for making such poor provision for his family, she defended him with vigor:

"Old as I am," she writes, "since I have taken my husband 'for better for worse,' I'll take my residence with him. Where he lives, will I live; and where he dies, will I die; and there will I be buried. God do so unto me, and more also, if aught but death part him and me. Confinement is nothing to one that, by sickness, is compelled to spend great part of her time in a chamber. And I sometimes think that, if it were not on account of Mr. Wesley and the children, it would be perfectly indifferent to my soul, whether she ascended to the Supreme Origin of being from a jail or a palace, for God is everywhere: Nor walls, nor locks, nor bars, nor deepest shade, nor closest solitude excludes his presence; and in what place soever he vouchsafes to manifest his presence, that place is heaven. And that man whose heart is penetrated with divine love, and enjoys the manifestations of God's blissful presence, is happy, let his outward condition be what it will. He is rich as having nothing, yet possessing all things. This world, this present state of things, is but for a time. What is now future will be present, as what is already past one was. And then, as Pascal observes, a little earth thrown on our cold head will forever determine our hopes and our condition. Nor will it signify much who personated the prince or the beggar, since, with respect to the exterior, all must stand on the same level after death."[14]

Susanna found her work arduous and trying; but she encouraged herself with thoughts of the future:

Though the education of so many children must create abundance of trouble, and will perpetually keep the mind employed as well as the body; yet consider 'tis no small honour to be entrusted with the care of so many souls. And if that trust be but managed with prudence and integrity, the harvest will abundantly recompense the toil of the seed-time; and it will be certainly no little accession to the future glory to stand forth at the last day and say, "'Lord, here are the children which Thou hast given me, of whom I have lost none by my ill example, nor by neglecting to instill into their minds, in their early years, the principles of Thy true religion and virtue!'"[15]

Look at your possessions, believer, and compare your portion with the circumstances of your friends. Some of them have their portion in the field; they are rich, and their harvests yield them a golden increase; but what are harvests compared with your God, who is the God of harvests? What are bursting granaries compared with Him who feeds you with the bread of heaven? Some have their portion in the city; their wealth is abundant and flows to them in constant streams until they become a very reservoir of gold; but what is gold compared with your God? You could not live on it; your spiritual life could not be sustained by it. Could it grant peace to a troubled conscience? Apply it to a sad heart, and see if it could prevent a single groan or minimize one grief.

But you have God, and in Him you have more than gold or riches could ever buy. Some have their portion in something most men love—applause and fame; but ask yourself, is not your God more to you than that? Do you think that human accolades or thunderous applause could prepare you to face death or encourage you in the prospect of judgment? No! There are sorrows in life that wealth cannot alleviate; and there is the deep need of a dying hour, for which no riches can provide.

But when you have God for your portion, you have more than everything else put together. In Him every need is met, whether in life or in death. With God for your portion you are rich indeed, for He will supply your need, comfort your heart, relieve your grief, guide your steps, walk with you in the dark valley, and then take you home to enjoy Him as your portion forever.

"I have enough," said Esau; this is the best thing a worldly man can say, but Jacob replied in essence, "I have everything," which is a note too high for carnal minds.

—Charles Spurgeon, "You Are Rich Indeed,"
Evening and Morning

WIDOWED

Year after difficult year passed in the Epworth rectory. Susanna and Samuel saw their surviving children enter adulthood. Samuel pressed on in his futile efforts to keep ahead of his debts:

As his health slowly failed, Samuel continued to work on his lifelong project: a book called *Dissertations on the Book of Job*. Though Samuel had hoped that its publication would assure his family's financial security, it did not prove so. Written in Latin, the ponderous and scholarly account did not appeal to the average reader. Samuel could possibly have been more successful by writing shorter and more popular pieces, but he preferred to devote his talents to what he considered a high level of scholarship.[16]

After Samuel passed away on April 5, 1735, Susanna was arrested for his debt. Dallimore comments that "we must assume that Samuel applied to the society for the relief of needy clergymen's widows, but there is no evidence that she received anything from that body. But 'Samuel Wesley tells John (Wesley) on April 29 that he has paid £30 to save his mother, who had been arrested for debt."[17]

My son, do not despise the *chastening* of the Lord, nor be discouraged when you are rebuked by him. For the Lord *disciplines* the one he loves, and *chastises* every son whom he receives. (Hebrews 12:5–6)

All believers need afflictions. It must be so, for the God of infinite love and wisdom *appoints* them, and His judgment can never err.

Saints are the *children* of God, but they need correction and discipline, etc.

The *precious seed* requires the use of the winnowing fan to blow away the chaff. So do saints.

The *gold* requires the furnace to purge away the dross. Saints are the gold which belongs to the King of the Church, and He places His gold in *the furnace of affliction* to purge away the dross of sin.

The *patient* requires medicine to restore to health—and God chastens His people to restore them to spiritual health.

Afflictions are needful to wean us from earth—and to induce us to aspire after Heaven!

Our fathers disciplined us for a little while as they thought best; but God disciplines us for our good, that we may share in His holiness. No discipline seems pleasant at the time, but painful. Later on, however, it produces a harvest of righteousness and peace for those who have been trained by it. Hebrews 12:10–11

Yet afflictions are *transient,* and will soon end. The end of our mortal life will be the end of all our sorrows. The *night of affliction* may appear long, but a *morning of joy* will follow it, which will be as long as eternity! It is a short night of sorrow—before a day of endless rejoicing.

At death sin dies, and sorrow expires! Sin is the mother—and *sorrow* is the daughter. The mother and daughter die on one bed, and are buried in one grave!

—William Nicholson, from a sermon (1862)
called "The Presence of God in Affliction"

After John had paid his father's debts, Susanna had very little. For the rest of her life she would depend on her children.[18]

Joni Eareckson Tada knows suffering in a way most of us will never understand. She has been a quadriplegic for over forty years, unable to move from the neck down. She writes:

I sure hope I can bring this wheelchair to heaven.

Now, I know that's not theologically correct.

But I hope to bring it and put it in a little corner of heaven, and then in my new, perfect, glorified body, standing on grateful glorified legs, I'll stand next to my Savior, holding his nail-pierced hands.

I'll say, "Thank you, Jesus," and he will know that I mean it, because he knows me.

He'll recognize me from the fellowship we're now sharing in his sufferings. And I will say,

"Jesus, do you see that wheelchair? You were right when you said that in this world we would have trouble,

because that thing was a lot of trouble. But the weaker
I was in that thing, the harder I leaned on you. And the
harder I leaned on you, the stronger I discovered you to be.
It never would have happened had you not given me the
bruising of the blessing of that wheelchair."

Then the real ticker-tape parade of praise will begin.
And all of earth will join in the party. And at that point
Christ will open up our eyes to the great fountain of joy
in his heart for us beyond all that we ever experienced on
earth.

And when we're able to stop laughing and crying, the
Lord Jesus really will wipe away our tears. I find it so poignant
that finally at the point when I do have the use of my arms to
wipe away my own tears, I won't have to, because God will.[19]

In all our trials we would do well to remember what Thomas Brooks
said in his sermon on remembering the *patience* of Job. It is *not*:
"Remember the *murmuring* of Job,
the *cursing* of Job,
the *complainings* of Job,
the *impatience* of Job," but
"Remember the *patience* of Job."
God looks upon the *pearl*—and not upon the *spot* that
is in it!

Just so, in Hebrews 11:30, 31, there is mention made of
Rahab's faith, love, and kind behavior towards the spies—
but no mention is made of her *lie* or *immorality*. The Lord
overlooks her *weakness*—and keeps His eye upon her *virtues*.

Where God sees but a little grace, He does, as it were,
hide His eyes from those circumstances that might seem to
deface the glory of it.

When the Lord comes to look upon a poor soul, He
lays His finger upon the scar, upon the infirmity—that He
may see nothing but grace, which is the beauty and the
glory of the soul.

"You are altogether beautiful, My love; there is no flaw
in you!" Song of Songs 4:7.

—from a sermon about Job by Puritan Thomas Brooks

Puritan Prayer[20]

Lord Jesus, I sin. Grant that I may never cease grieving because of it, never be content with myself, never think I can reach a point of perfection. Kill my envy, command my tongue, trample down self. Give me grace to be holy, kind, gentle, pure, peaceable, to live for thee and not for self, to copy thy words, acts, spirit, to be transformed into thy likeness, to be consecrated wholly to thee, to live entirely to thy glory.

Deliver me from attachment to things unclean, from wrong associations, from the predominance of evil passions, from the sugar of sin as well as its gap; that with self-loathing, deep contrition, earnest heart-searching I may come to thee, cast myself on thee, trust in thee, cry to thee, be delivered by thee.

O God, the Eternal All, help me to know that all things are shadows, but thou art substance, all things are quicksands, but thou art mountain, all things are shifting, but thou art anchor, all things are ignorance, but thou art wisdom.

If my life is to be a crucible amid burning heat, so be it, but do thou sit at the furnace mouth to watch the ore that nothing be lost. If I sin wilfully, grievously, tormentedly, in grace take away my mourning and give me music; remove my sackcloth and clothe me with beauty; still my sighs and fill my mouth with song, then give me summer weather as a Christian. Amen.

CHAPTER 6
SUSANNA'S RELIANCE ON PRAYER

S USANNA WESLEY was in the habit of taking her needs to the Lord in prayer. She definitely lived up to the modern term, "prayer warrior." By all accounts, she recognized prayer as being one of her greatest weapons, and took to heart scriptural verses on prayer such as these:

> The Lord is nigh unto all them that call upon him, to all that call upon him in truth. (Psalm 145:18)

> And this is the confidence that we have in him, that, if we ask any thing according to his will, he heareth us. (1 John 5:14)

Praying was like breathing for Susanna, and her tremendous faith in God was clearly demonstrated through her prayer life. Among her many prayers, here is one:

> O God, I find it most difficult to preserve a devout and serious temper of mind in the midst of much worldly business. Were I permitted to choose a state of life, or positively to ask of Thee anything in this world, I would humbly choose and beg that I might have daily bread with moderate care and that I might have more leisure to retire from the world without injuring those dependent on me. Yet I do not know whether such a state of life would really be best for me; nor am I assured that if I had more leisure I should be more zealously devoted to Thee and serve

Thee better than now.[1]

In this prayer, we feel her pouring out her heart to the Lord. We can hear her being vulnerable when she expresses that there is a battle between having to care for people and things, and wanting to have more time for the Lord. Then she expresses a real fear that if she had more time, she might spend it on other things, things that are vain and of less value. This is the battle that we face as Christians. Our life is lived in tension.

As mentioned in chapter 2, Puritan Richard Baxter was friends with Susanna's father, and he spent time in their home. She very well may have sat in on their theological discussions, as she was very well-read in theological matters. It is said that her sister and other siblings had a hard time getting her nose out of books about God or a textbook about languages. Her father's library had a great assortment of Puritan writings, and her devotional journals reveal the enduring influence of Richard Baxter on her life. Baxter is known to have said the following, and for all we know he said it in her presence: "Make careful choice of the books which you read: let the Holy Scriptures ever have the preeminence. . . . Let Scripture be first and most in your hearts and hands and other books be used as subservient to it."[2] He suggested that while reading, a Christian should ask himself or herself:

1. Could I spend this time no better?

2. Are there better books that would edify me more?

3. Are the lovers of such a book as this the greatest lovers of the Book of God and of a holy life?

4. Does this book increase my love to the Word
   of God, kill my sin, and prepare me for the life
   to come?

Truly, "The words of the wise are like goads, their collected sayings like firmly embedded nails—given by one Shepherd. Be warned, my son, of anything in addition to them. Of making many books there is no end, and much study wearies the body" (Ecclesiastes 12:11–12).

Here is another line from Baxter on prayer: "Prayer is the breath of the new creature."[3]

At one time while suffering from a very serious illness, Richard Baxter set his thoughts on heaven and he wrote a book entitled, *The Saints Everlasting Rest,* in which he sought to stir up the hearts of his hearers for meditation on heaven and actively pursuing the Lord through prayer.

The book, written in 1650, has been recognized as Baxter's most famous work. This means that it would have been circulated in Susanna's father's circle and was no doubt part of his large library. In Baxter's own lifetime the book reached twelve editions, until it was first abridged and published in that form by Susanna's son John Wesley in 1754. Here is a prime excerpt from the book, from one of Baxter's excellent sermons on prayer:

Now, reader, according to the directions already given, conscientiously practice meditation as well as prayer. Do it daily if possible. Retire into some private place at the most convenient time, and lay aside all worldly thoughts. With all possible seriousness and reverence look up towards heaven. Remember there is your everlasting rest. Study its excellency and reality. Rise from sense to faith by comparing heavenly with earthly joys. Then mix exclamations with your soliloquies, until, having pleaded the case reverently with God and seriously with your own heart, you have ignited yourself from dust to flame. It will change you from a forgetful sinner and lover of the world, to an ardent lover of God; from a fearful coward to a persistent Christian; from an unfruitful sadness to a joyful life. In other words, this activity will wean your heart from earth to heaven; from crawling in earth's dust to walking with God.

As you meditate on your everlasting rest, here are some suggestions. Consider the significance of "rest." How sweet the sound. Rest! Not as the stone that rests on the earth. Not as this flesh shall rest in the grave. But that active rest, when we "rest not day and night, saying, Holy, holy, holy Lord God Almighty!" (Rev. 4:8). When we shall rest from sin, but not from worship; from suffering and sorrow, but not from joy. O blessed day, when I shall rest with God. My perfect soul and body shall together perfectly enjoy the most perfect God; when God, who is Love itself, shall perfectly love me.

Consider how near that rest is. Though my Lord seems to delay His coming, yet a little while and He will be here. What are a few hundred years when they are over? I think I hear His trumpet sound. I think I see Him coming in the clouds, with His attending angels, in majesty and glory.

Now, blessed saints, that have believed and obeyed, this is the climax of faith and patience. This is it for which you prayed and waited. Are you now sorry for your sufferings and sorrows, your self-sacrifices and holy living? See how the Judge smiles on you; there is love in His looks, the titles of Redeemer, Husband, Head, are written in His friendly, shining face. Listen! He calls you. He invites you to stand on His right hand. Fear not, for that is where He sets His sheep. O happy announcement, "Come you blessed of my Father, inherit the kingdom prepared for you from the foundation of the world" (Matt. 25:34). He takes you by the hand, the door is open, the kingdom is His and therefore yours; there is your place before His throne. The Father receives you as the spouse of his Son, and bids you welcome. Ever so unworthy, you must be crowned. This was the purpose of free redeeming grace, the climax of eternal love. O blessed grace; O wonderful love! But I cannot express it. I cannot even imagine it.

This is that joy which was purchased by sorrow, that crown which was bought by the cross. My Lord wept, that now my tears might be wiped away. He bled, that I might now rejoice. He was forsaken, that I might have this fellowship. He then died, that I might now live. O free mercy, that can exalt so unworthy a sinner. Free to me, though costly to Christ!

This is not like our cottages of clay, our prisons, our earthly dwellings. This voice of joy is not like our old complaints, our impatient groans and sighs; nor this harmonious praise like the curses which we heard on earth. This body is not like what we had, nor this soul like the soul we had, nor this life like the life we lived. Where are the old divisions, arguments, bad names, exasperated tempers, frowns, and uncharitable condemnations? Now we are all of one heart, home, and happiness. O sweet reconciliation! Now the Gospel shall no more be dishonored through our foolishness. No more, my soul, shall you mourn for suffering friends, nor weep over their graves. You shall never suffer your old temptations from Satan, the world, or your own flesh. Your pains and sickness are all cured. Your body shall no more burden you with weakness and weariness. Headaches and hunger, insomnia and exhaustion, all are gone. Blessed change! Farewell sin and sorrow forever. Good-bye my proud, unbelieving heart—my worldly, sensual, carnal mind; and welcome now my most holy, heavenly nature. My face will not wrinkle, nor my hair be gray; for this corruptible shall have put on incorruption, and this mortal, immortality, and death shall be swallowed up in victory. "O death, where is your sting? O grave, where is your victory?" (1 Cor. 15:54-55). The date of my lease will no more expire. When millions of ages are passed, my glory is but beginning; and when millions more are passed, it is no nearer ending.

Ah, drowsy, earthly heart, how coldly do you think of this coming day. Would you rather sit down in dirt than walk in the palace of God? Is it better to be here, than above with God? Is the company better? Are the pleasures greater? Yonder is your Father's glory. Yonder, O my soul, must you go when you depart this body. When the power of your Lord raises your body and joins you to your new immortal body, yonder you will live with God forever. There is the glorious New Jerusalem, the gates of pearl, the foundation of pearl, the streets and sidewalks of transparent gold.

O my soul, do you stagger at the promises of God through unbelief? (Romans 4:20). I highly suspect you. If you really believed, you would be more excited by it. Is it not under the signature and oath of God? Can God lie? Can He that is Truth itself be false? What need does God have to flatter or deceive you? Why should He promise you more than He will perform? Dare not to charge the wise, Almighty, faithful God with this! O wretched heart of unbelief, has God made you a promise of rest, and will you come short of it? Your eyes and ears and all your senses may prove delusions sooner than a promise of God could delude you. You may be more certain of that which is written in the Word, than if you saw it with your own eyes or felt it with your own hands.

As I cannot match the Lord in works of power, no more can I match Him in love. Lord, I surrender. I am completely overcome by thy love. Thy captive will gladly proclaim thy victory. Shall I not love at all, because I cannot reach thine immeasurable love? Though I cannot say that I love thee as thou lovest me, yet I can say, "Lord, thou knowest that I want to love thee. I am angry with my heart that it does not love thee more."

My Lord has taught me to rejoice in hope of His glory, and even to see it through the present bars of a prison—for, when "persecuted for righteousness' sake," He commands me to "rejoice, and be exceeding glad," because "my reward in heaven is great" (Matt. 5:10-12).

But thy feast, my Lord, is nothing to me without an appetite. Thou hast set the delicacies of heaven before me; but unfortunately, I am blind and cannot see them. I am sick and cannot relish them. I am so paralyzed that I cannot put forth a hand to take them. I therefore, humbly beg this grace, that as thou hast opened heaven to me in thy word, so *thou* wouldst open my eyes to see it, and my heart to delight in it. O Spirit of life, breathe thy grace into me. Take me by the hand, and lift me from the earth, that may see what glory thou hast prepared for those who love thee (1 Corinthians 2:9–10).

Can my tongue say that I shall shortly and surely live with God, and yet my heart not leap within me? Can I say it with faith, and not with joy? Ah, faith, how clearly do I now see your weakness. But though unbelief darkens my light, and dulls my life, and suppresses my joys; it shall not be able to conquer and destroy me. Can beautiful objects delight my eyes, or pleasant odors my smell, or melody my ears; and shall not the forethought of celestial bliss delight me?

Lord, thou hast reserved my perfect joy for heaven. Help me to desire until I may possess, and let me long for it when I cannot, as I wish I could, rejoice in it.

Why do I so easily forget my resting place? O my soul, does the dullness of your desire after rest not accuse you of most detestable ingratitude and foolishness? Must your Lord purchase you a rest at so costly a price, and you not value it more? Must he go before to prepare so glorious a mansion for such a wretch, and are you reluctant to go and possess it? Shall the Lord of glory desire your company, and you do not desire his? Must earth become a very hell to you before you are willing to be with God? If your successful efforts and godly friends seem better to you than a life with God, it is time for God to take them from you.

Ah, my dear Lord, though I cannot say, "My soul longs after thee" (Psalm 84:2), yet I can say, "I long for such a longing heart." "The spirit is willing, but the flesh is weak" (Matt. 26:4). My spirit cries, "Let 'thy kingdom come' (Matt. 6:10), or let me come to thy kingdom;" but the flesh is afraid you might hear my prayer and take me at my word!

I am willing to stay here on earth while thou wouldst use me. Give me the work which thou hast for my hands. But when it is done, take me at my best. I don't want to be so impatient as to ask thee to cut off my time and take me home before I am prepared, for I know my eternal reward depends so much on the use I make of this life. But neither would

I stay here when my work is done. While I must be absent from thee, let my soul as sincerely groan as my body does when it is sick.

O Savior, hasten the time of thy return. Let that joyful trumpet sound the signal for the great resurrection day, when thy command shall go forth, and none disobey. Then the sea and the earth shall yield up their hostages, and all that sleep in the grave shall awaken, and the dead in Christ shall rise first. I can lay down my body in the dust, trusting it not to a grave, but to thee, O Lord. Therefore shall my flesh rest in hope, until thou shalt raise it to everlasting rest.

O let "thy kingdom come" (Matt. 6:10). Thy homesick bride says, "Come!" for thy Spirit within her says, "Come!" and teaches her thus to pray (Revelation 22:17). Yes, the whole creation says, "Come!" And thou thyself have said, "Surely I come quickly. Amen. Even so, come, Lord Jesus" (Rev. 22:20).[4]

Christians know that "the effectual fervent prayer of a righteous man availeth much" (James 5:16), and Susanna certainly had much to accomplish with a house full of children not only to raise and educate largely on her own, but at times to provide for as well.

When Susanna was young, she promised the Lord that for every hour she spent in entertainment, she would give another hour to Him in prayer and in the Word. Taking care of the house and raising so many children made this commitment nearly impossible to fulfill as she had no time for either entertainment or long hours in prayer. Instead, she worked the gardens, milked the cows, schooled the children and managed the entire house herself. In a compromise of sorts, she decided instead to give the Lord two hours a day in prayer.[5]

Two hours a day! What a tremendous amount of time, but time very well spent, as much of what she desired in life was accomplished through the means of prayer, such as God using her son John in such a mighty way as the "Father of Methodism," and her son Charles also becoming a preacher and a prolific hymn-writer. "With special love she watched over the soul of the boy whose narrow escape from death had more endeared him to her. Surely he had been spared that he might do some great good work, for which it might be her privilege to prepare him. Her toil was not wasted."[6] We can safely assume that she prayed earnestly for her children to serve and love the Lord.

No doubt Susanna struggled to find a secret place to get away with God, as her "prayer closet" was always full of children, as she would have up to thirteen pairs of eyes clamoring for her attention at one point. She told her children that when they saw her with her apron over her head, that meant she was in prayer and was therefore not to be disturbed. Some have likened her to a surgeon who is fully dressed in surgical scrubs, gloves, and mask standing over a patient performing open heart surgery. No one would dare tap the surgeon on the shoulder during such an important procedure to ask him for anything. Such a break in concentration could be costly to the patient's life, and clearly,

Susanna felt any such break would be very costly to her prayer life.

Much of the two hours a day she spent praying was centered on praying for her children. One can readily imagine the great impact such an obvious display of prayer and communion had on all of them as they saw her diligently seeking the Lord day after day. Even the youngest of the children would have noticed their father's regular absence from the home, and how their mother consistently sought help from her heavenly Father to sustain them. Even though the children could not disturb her during her prayer time, one wonders if she ever prayed out loud so that they heard prayers like this one:

> Help me, O Lord, to make a true use of all disappointments and calamities in this life, in such wise that they may unite my heart more closely with thee. Cause them to separate my affections from worldly things and inspire my soul with more vigour in the pursuit of true happiness.[7]

Listen to her tough realism in these words:

> Since I must expect to meet with many difficulties, much opposition, many disappointments and daily trials of faith and patience in my passage through this world, may it be my highest wisdom to disengage my affections as much as I lawfully may from all transitory, temporal enjoyments, and to fix them on those more rational and spiritual pleasures which we are to enjoy when we enter upon our state of immortality.[8]

Listen to her wisdom, won by many years of difficulty, in these words: "The best preparation I know of for suffering is a regular and exact performance of present duty.[9]

Later in her life Susanna prayed,

> Help me, Lord, to remember that religion is not to be confined to the church, or closet, nor exercised only in prayer and meditation, but that everywhere I am in thy presence. So may my every word and action have a moral content. . . . May all the happenings of my life prove useful and beneficial to me. May all things instruct me and afford me an opportunity of exercising some virtue and daily learning and growing toward thy likeness. . . . Amen.[10]

What a bold prayer! Instead of saying, "Lord, keep me from all trials," she acknowledged that trials will come, and even welcomed them as a way to grow closer to God and to be conformed more to His likeness. The only way to pray such a prayer with complete faith is to start with a right understanding of who God is; He is good, sovereign, and unchangeable, and He has been the same since before the Creation. After He made human beings and everything else in the world, He declared all things to be "very good," something He could not have declared unless "good" was part of who He is. Because He is good, He does all things for *our* good.

Susanna would have been familiar with Romans 8:28, which reads, "And we know that all things work together for good to them that love God, to them who are the called according to his purpose." Through His providence He works everything in our lives, good and bad, for our good and His glory. Only because God is good are we able to rest in His sovereignty, for if He were not good we would not trust Him with anything in our lives. Instead, He *is* good and sovereign and unchangeable. Even when we are in our lowest valleys, the truth remains that God is still on the throne and sovereign over all.

ON FAMILY PRAYER

Annesley family friend, Puritan Richard Baxter, said, "Let family worship be performed consistently and at a time when it is most likely for the family to be free of interruptions"[11] as one of the greatest joys for a Christian family is to pray together. Regularly coming together as a family teaches our children to be more thankful for the Giver than the gifts, and teaches them to keep their focus fully where it belongs, on God and God alone.

As anyone with a toddler knows, children tend to put their wants and desires first, so they must be taught at a very young age to put God and others before themselves, which is critically important, and something Susanna Wesley did. "She associated her children with family worship before they could speak; their first lispings were in words of prayer; they quickly learned to honor the Lord's day; and the elder were enlisted in the work of instructing the younger in Scripture truth."[12] John Wesley, writing in his journal, gives us a glimpse into their daily routine for praying as a family:

Daily Family Prayer:
At six, as soon as family prayers were over, they had their supper; at seven, the maid washed them;

and, beginning at the youngest, she undressed and got them all to bed by eight; at which time she left them in their several rooms awake; for there was no such thing allowed of in our house, as sitting by a child till it fell asleep.

Children taught to pray early:

The children of this family were taught, as soon as they could speak, the Lord's prayer, which they were made to say at rising and bed-time constantly; to which, as they grew bigger, were added a short prayer for their parents, and some collects; a short catechism, and some portion of Scripture, as their memories could bear.

They were very early made to distinguish the Sabbath from other days; before they could well speak or go. They were as soon taught to be still at family prayers, and to ask a blessing immediately after, which they used to do by signs, before they could kneel or speak.[13]

The great effects of such a diligent routine of teaching Christian character were most noticed when the routine was suddenly lost like on that dreadful day, February 9, 1709. After the fire at the rectory, in which six-year-old John nearly lost his life, the Wesleys barely had but one pound between them and it was determined that the family was going to have to be split up and the children dispersed to different families.

Thankfully, Mr. Wesley did not dally in rebuilding and by the year's end his scattered family were reunited. . . But the little ones, deprived of their mother's mild, firm governance, were fast learning the rough, coarse ways of the neighbors among whom they had been dispersed, forgetting the sweet, pure, wholesome thoughts and habits of their home. To find them thus degenerated seemed to Mrs. Wesley the saddest result of that disastrous fire. To remedy the evil, she encouraged them in new religious observances, causing them to engage more frequently and regularly in prayer, in praise, in private study of the Scriptures.[14]

Later, Susanna wrote something similar to her son Samuel (Sammy) when he was at Westminster with his father,

Dear Sammy,

"Let your light so shine before men that they may see your good works and glorify your Father which is in heaven."

Examine well your heart, and observe its inclinations, particularly what the general temper of your mind is; for, let me tell you, it is not a fit of devotion now and then speaks a man a Christian, but it is a mind universally and generally disposed to all the duties of Christianity in their proper times, places, &c. For instance, in the morning or evening or any other time when occasion is offered a good Christian will be cheerfully disposed to retire from the world that he may offer to his Creator his sacrifice of prayer and praise and will account it his happiness as well as his duty, so to do. When he is in the world, if he have business he will follow it diligently as knowing that he must account with God at night for what he has done in the day. And that God expects we should be faithful in our calling as well as devout in our closets. A Christian ought, and in the general does, converse with the world like a stranger in an inn. He will use what is necessary for him and cheerfully enjoy what he innocently can; but at the same time he knows it is but an inn and he will be but little concerned with what he meets with there because he takes it not for his home. The mind of a Christian should be always composed, temperate, free from all extremes of mirth or sadness, and always disposed to hear the still small voice of God's Holy Spirit, which will direct him what and how to act in all the occurrences of life, if in all his ways he acknowledge him and depend on his assistance.[15]

ANSWERED PRAYERS

Our gracious and kind God not only listens to our prayers, but He also answers them. When we go humbly before God with our prayers and petitions, desiring Him to answer according to His will, we are praying as Christ prayed in Luke 22:42 when he said, "nevertheless not my will, but thine, be done."

What a great encouragement when we see His will and ours in perfect alignment. Answered prayers strengthen our resolve to keep persevering in our trials, and help us to stay focused on the prize, which is Christ. Seeing the answered prayers of others has the same effect.

As the death of her husband approached, Susanna drew

on the strength of this truth:

> As the spring came on, the Rector became weaker, and at length, feeling sure that the end was near, Mrs. Wesley sent for John and Charles. They came in time for him to enjoy seeing them and talking with them; and as they watched him, they observed how his most cherished aspirations were given up at the approach of death. These were the desire of finishing *Job,* of paying his debts and of seeing his eldest son once more in the flesh. Emelia came over from Gainsborough, where her brothers had enabled her to set up a school for herself; and they took turns in watching and tending him. Mrs. Wesley was thoroughly broken down, and came into the room but rarely, for she invariably fainted and had to be carried away and restored by those whose hands were already so full. Mr. Wesley passed peacefully away at sunset on April 25, 1735 sensible to the end, drawing his last breath as his son John finished repeating the commendatory prayer for the second time. They went immediately to tell their mother, who was less affected than they feared she would have been, and said that her prayers were heard in his having so easy a death and her being so strengthened to bear it.[16]

Another answer to prayer occurred in response to the fire at the Epworth rectory, when the child John Wesley had been left for lost in the building after his agonized father had been repeatedly beaten back by the flames:

> As the Rector, kneeling in prayer in an outer passage, commended to God the soul of the lad,

whom he thought surely doomed, kindly neighbors formed a human pyramid which was the means of the lad's rescue. To John, the mystic, that prayer always seemed to be the divine seal on a peculiar and exalted mission for which he had been miraculously preserved. His tombstone he ordered to be inscribed, "A brand plucked out of the burning." In the rescue his mother saw an equal miracle. She encouraged John's belief in his great destiny and fostered his high hope. "What shall I render unto the Lord for his mercies? The little unworthy praise that I can offer is so mean and contemptible an offering, that I am even ashamed to tender it. But, Lord, accept it for the sake of Christ, and pardon the deficiency of the sacrifice. I would offer thee myself, and all that thou hast given me; and I would resolve—O give me grace to do it!—that the residue of my life shall be all devoted to thy service. And I do intend to be more particularly careful of the soul of this child, that thou hast so mercifully provided for, than ever I have been; that I may endeavor to instill into his mind the principles of thy true religion and virtue. Lord, give me grace to do it sincerely and prudently; and bless my attempts with good success." The answer to this prayer was Methodism.[17]

The epistle of James reminds us of the many injunctions in Scripture about prayer. The burden and the need to pray is rooted in the mandate of prayer, and prayer is commanded of the believer because the impulse to pray is the natural by-product of regeneration. Augustine is famous for saying, "Lord give what you command and command what You

SUSANNA WESLEY: HER REMARKABLE LIFE

will." And it was the Puritan William Gurnall who said:

> Praying is the same to the new creature as crying is to the natural. The child is not learned by art or example to cry, but instructed by nature; it comes into the world crying. Praying is not a lesson got by forms and rules of art, but flowing from principles of the new life itself.[18]

I am no longer my own but thine,
   Put me to what thou wilt.
   Put me to doing, put me to suffering.
   Let me be employed for thee or laid aside for thee.
   Let me be full, let me be empty.
   Let me have all things, let me have nothing.
   I freely and wholeheartedly yield all things to thy pleasure and disposal.
   And now glorious and blessed God, Father, Son and Holy Spirit, thou art mine and I am thine. So be it. And this covenant now made on earth, let it be satisfied in heaven.
   Amen.[19]

—John Wesley

Lead Me

   Preserve me from all those snares and temptations which continually solicit me to offend thee. Guide me by thy Holy Spirit in all those places whither thy Providence shall lead me this day, and suffer not my communications with the world to dissipate my thoughts, to make me inadvertent to thy presence or luke warm in thy service. But let me always walk as in thy sight, and as one who knows this life to be the seed-time of an eternal harvest.
   Amen.

—John Wesley

PURITAN PRAYER[20]

O Lord, in prayer I launch far out into the eternal world, and on that broad ocean my soul triumphs over all evils on the shores of mortality. Time, with its gay amusements and cruel disappointments never appears so inconsiderate as then.

In prayer I see myself as nothing; I find my heart going after Thee with intensity, and long with vehement thirst to live to Thee. Blessed be the strong gales of the Spirit that speed me on my way to the New Jerusalem.

In prayer all things here below vanish, and nothing seems important but holiness of heart and the salvation of others.

In prayer all my worldly cares, fears, anxieties disappear, and are of as little significance as a puff of wind.

In prayer my soul inwardly exults with lively thoughts at what Thou art doing for Thy church, and I long that Thou shouldest get thyself a great name from sinners returning to Zion.

In prayer I am lifted above the frowns and flatteries of life, and taste heavenly joys; entering into the eternal world I can give myself to Thee with all my heart, to be Thine for ever.

In prayer I can place all my concerns in Thy hands, to be entirely at Thy disposal, having no will or interest of my own.

In prayer I can intercede for my friends, ministers, sinners, the church, Thy kingdom to come, with greatest freedom, ardent hopes, as a son to his father, as a lover to the beloved.

Help me to be all prayer and never to cease praying.

Amen.

CHAPTER 7
SUSANNA'S CONVERSION— TRUE OR FALSE?

A CLOSE STUDY of the life of Susanna Wesley causes some difference of opinion about when she was saved. Naturally, while some people can recount the exact moment in time when they were saved, others, while they do not doubt their conversion, cannot point to any particular moment when they passed from death to life. People who have been raised in a Christian home where they grew up knowing the fear of God and had the teachings of Scripture from birth may not have a particular moment in time when there was a clear and definite change in their life. But God opens the eyes of other people on a specific day, which makes it is easier for them to be sure of their salvation because they can remember when, where, and how it happened, and can see a definite change in their lives.

One incident occurred on a Sunday in 1739 that made John and Charles Wesley both believe that their mother might have been saved later in life. She had a "strong sense of forgiveness," as she received the cup from her son-in-law, the Rev. Wesley Hall, and she reported it to her son John. The Introduction to *Susanna Wesley: The Complete Writings* explains further:

> She spoke to him [John] of the strong sense of forgiveness she felt while receiving the cup from her son-in-law Hall at Communion one Sunday in August

91

1739. Though John and Charles both made a bit too much of the incident, "assurance of pardon" being an expected mark of Methodist experience, and though she would have been scandalized had she known of Hall's unfaithfulness to her daughter, which came out only later, Susanna was genuinely touched.[1]

History tells us that Samuel Annesley (Susanna's father), often declared that he did not remember the time when he was not converted. Having grown up in a godly family, he must have been surrounded by the teachings of Scripture. And this was the case with Susanna too. We know that Samuel Annesley feared the Lord, and we know that he raised her in the ways of the Lord. All the Puritans respected him. But because her son, Charles, himself found peace with God and consequently believed that other people, like him, must possess knowledge of an exact moment of internal change as an essential sign of true salvation, he felt that his mother should have such a definite experience too. Repeatedly, he and his mother wrote about it in their letters to each other. Her typical responds was, "I do not judge it necessary to know the precise time of our conversion."[2]

What we know from Susanna's life is that from her earliest childhood years she loved reading books having to do with the things of God and that she would not spend more time in amusement than she spent in meditation and prayer. All her life, she paid strict attention to spiritual things, she cared about the lost (such as her son Samuel, whom she didn't think had been converted), and she had a prayerful spirit (not just for herself, but also for others).

Once when her eldest son Samuel felt doubtful about

his election from Westminster to an Oxford scholarship, she advised him to "beg God's favour in this great affair;" and she recommended to him: "If you can possibly, set apart two hours of Sunday afternoon, from four to six, for this employment, which time I also have determined to the same work."[3] It appears that she must have had a relationship with the Lord to be willing and able to spend two hours in prayer and to care so much about the Lord's guidance. This doesn't seem like something an unbeliever would do. However, we know that people can engage in religious activities, making all sorts of prayers and spending hours devoted in religious duties, yet be doing it to please themselves or someone else. Was Susanna's motivation religious duty or a truly converted heart?

Kirk writes about the extent of her devotion to prayer. He says that "Two hours of the day, one in the morning and another in the evening, with an occasional interval at noon, were consecrated to secret communion with God." Kirk goes on to say that her times in prayer were solemn acts of worship and that she "charged herself to take, at least, a quarter of an hour to collect and compose her thoughts before she attempted to approach the throne of grace."[4]

Susanna herself said more about this:

> If but some earthly prince, or some person of eminent quality were certainly to visit you, or you were to visit him, would you not be careful to have your apparel and all about you decent, before you came into his presence? How much more should you take care to have your mind in order, when you take upon yourself the honour to speak to the Sovereign

Lord of the Universe! Upon the temper of the soul, in your addresses to Him, depends your success in a very great measure. He is infinitely too great to be trifled with; too wise to be imposed on by a mock devotion; and He abhors a sacrifice without a heart. An habitual sense of His perfections is an admirable help against cold and formal performances. Though the lamp of devotion is always burning, yet a wise virgin will arise and trim before going forth to meet the Bridegroom.[5]

Susanna also seemed to give great importance to self-examination. We read in the Bible: "Examine yourselves, whether ye be in the faith; prove your own selves. Know ye not your own selves, how that Jesus Christ is in you, except ye be reprobates?" (2 Corinthians 13:5). In other versions Christians are supposed to test themselves to see whether or not they are in the faith. We read in Lamentations 3:40, "Let us search and try our ways, and turn again to the Lord." And in 1 Corinthians 11:28 we read, "But let a man examine himself, and so let him eat of that bread, and drink of that cup." So we see that the Bible has a lot to say about examining ourselves. Sadly, too many Christians hesitate to examine themselves because they are afraid that they might find they are spiritually sick. The same is true of us going to the doctor. Many people do not want to see a physician for a yearly checkup because they would rather be ignorant than to find out that something is wrong.

Ignorance can be deadly. And not testing yourself to see whether you are in the faith can be spiritually deadly. Here are nine evidences (adapted from John MacArthur's

Commentary on 1 and 2 Thessalonians) by which you can test yourself by to see if you are in the faith. These are evidences that the church in Thessalonica possessed:

- A faith that works (see 1 Thessalonians 1:3a). A true saving belief in Jesus Christ will always result in a mighty work of God that produces change in a person's nature or disposition.

- A love that labors (see 1 Thessalonians 1:3b). True Christians minister out of the motivation of their love for others. Loving even one's enemies is an expression of the power of salvation.

- A hope that endures (see 1 Thessalonians 1:3c). All Christians have a hope in the Lord Jesus Christ—a persevering anticipation of seeing His future glory and receiving their eternal inheritance.

- A reception of the gospel in power and the Holy Spirit (see 1 Thessalonians 1:5).

- A genuine imitation of the Lord (see 1 Thessalonians 1:6a) "they became imitators of Paul and of the Lord...patterns of holy living immediately began replacing the old sinful ones."

- A joyful endurance in tribulation (see 1 Thessalonians 1:6b). No matter how difficult circumstances become, true Christians do not lose their ultimate joy because the Holy Spirit dispenses it to the elect.

- A proclamation of the Word everywhere (see 1 Thessalonians 1:8–9a). True Christians are faithful in the proclamation of the gospel message, far and wide.

- A total transformation from idolatry
  (see 1 Thessalonians 1:9b).

- An expectant looking for the return of Christ
  (see 1 Thessalonians 1:10).

Christians must keep short accounts with God. Then we can be in continual communion with Him. 1 John 1:9 tells us that "If we confess our sins, He is faithful and just to forgive us our sins, and to cleanse us from all unrighteousness." Make a habit of being in continual communication with the Lord whether you are traveling to work, taking care of daily affairs, eating dinner, or watching television.

Make up your spiritual accounts daily; see how matters stand between God and your souls (Psalm 77:6). Often reckonings keep God and conscience friends. Do with your hearts as you do with your watches, wind them up every morning by prayer, and at night examine whether your hearts have gone true all that day, whether the wheels of your affections have moved swiftly toward heaven.

When a man has judged himself, Satan is put out of office. When he lays anything to a saint's charge, he is able to retort and say, "It is true, Satan, I am guilty of these sins, but I have judged myself already for them; and having condemned myself in the lower court of conscience, God will acquit me in the upper court of heaven."

Self-examination is the setting up a court in conscience and keeping a register there, that by strict scrutiny a man may know how things stand between God and his own soul. Self-examination is a spiritual inquisition, a bringing one's self to trial. A good Christian doth as it were the day of Judgment here in his own soul. Self-searching is a heart-anatomy.

—Puritan Thomas Watson

Susanna determined to keep her "mind in a temper of recollection, often in the day calling it in from outward objects, lest it should wander into forbidden paths." She said, "Make an examination of your conscience at least three times a day, and omit no opportunity of retirement from the world."[6] She kept this pattern until sicknesses slowed down her pace and hampered her thinking.

In this quote from Susanna, we can see her deep self-examination"

You, above all others, have most need of humbling yourself before the great and holy God, for the very great and very many sins you daily are guilty of, in thought, word and deed, against His Divine Majesty. What an habitual levity is there in your thoughts! How many vain, impure thoughts pass through the mind in one hour! And though they do not take up the abode for any long continuance, yet their passing through often leaves a tincture of impurity. How many worldly regards, even in sacred actions, with habitual inadvertence; seldom any seriousness, or composure of spirit; the passions rude and tumultuous, very susceptible of violent impressions, from light and inconsiderable accidents, unworthy a reasonable being, but more unworthy a Christian. Keep thy heart with all diligence—thy thoughts, thy affections—for out of them are the issues of life. Who can tell how oft he offendeth in this kind? Oh cleanse Thou me from secret faults! Out of the abundance of the heart the mouth speaketh. How many unnecessary words are you guilty of daily? How many opportunities of speaking for the good of the souls committed to your care are neglected? How seldom do you speak of God with that reverence, that humility, that gravity that you ought? Your words, as well as your thoughts, are deficient. You do not conceive or speak of God aright. You do not speak magnificently or worthily of Him who is the high and lofty One that inhabiteth eternity, the Creator of the Universe![7]

Although evidence shows that she raised her children in the fear and admonition of the Lord, yet her sons John and Charles Wesley did not believe she was truly saved until later in life, close to the time when she was facing her death. English Puritan and theologian John Howe, who served briefly as a chaplain to Oliver Cromwell and who was a contemporary of Susanna, thought otherwise. He said of her: "Her assiduity in her religious course, the seasons, order and constancy whereof seemed to be governed by the ordinances of heaven, that ascertain the succession of day and night; so that . . . one might as soon divert the course of the sun, as turn from her daily course in religious duties; this argued a steady principle and of the highest excellency, that of Divine love."[8]

All of Susanna's sons left home to further their education when they were young. Her son, Samuel, at the young age of thirteen was sent off to school. John attended his mother's classes until the age of eleven, when he was sent off to school. Charles attended his mother's school until the age of nine, and then he left to attend the Westminster School. But even after they left, Susanna still continued to instruct them through letters about God and man and morals. Her eldest son, Sammy, was the one she tended to write to the most. In a letter she wrote to him after recovering from an illness, she reminds him:

I shall be employing my thoughts on useful subjects to you when I have time, for I desire nothing in this world so much as to have my children well instructed in the principles of religion, that they may walk in the narrow way which alone leads to happiness. Particularly I am concerned for you, who were, before your birth, dedicated to the service of the sanctuary, that you may be an ornament of that church of which you are a member.[9]

In a letter written to her son, John, she gives her approval over how he is conducting his life; except she points out one thing in him that was flawed in her eyes; he had not given himself enough to meditation. She certainly did. Her letters show that she was in deep prayer and meditation about lofty subjects such as the works of creation, the ways of the Lord, the human body, and the work of Christ.[10]

In her letters she expresses that the more she studies God and the older she gets, the less she knows. This is a true sign of a maturing Christian. She is like Paul, who started out his early letters calling himself an "apostle of the Lord Jesus Christ, but then changed his tone as he got older and wiser. Immediately before he was to depart and see the Lord, he was calling himself the "least of all the saints." Here is how Susanna expressed in her letters the following:

After so many years' inquiry, so long reading and so much thinking, His boundless essence seems more inexplicable, the perfection of His glory more bright and inaccessible. The farther I search the less

SUSANNA WESLEY: HER REMARKABLE LIFE

I discover; and I seem now more ignorant than when I first began to know something of him.[11]

In another letter to young Sammy, she talked about Scripture. She wrote: "Let your light so shine before men that they may see your good works, and glorify your Father which is in heaven." She continued by saying, "the mind of a Christian should always be composed, temperate, free from all extremes of mirth or sadness, and always disposed to hear the voice of God's Holy Spirit."[12]

She was also very temperate and self-controlled in terms of drinking alcohol. Because pure water was difficult to come by, most families would brew beer to make sure impurities were removed, and the Wesleys did this in their kitchen. But Susanna wrote to Sammy to ensure that he would not be given too much wine: "Writing to him on 22 May 1706 she stated, "Two glasses cannot hurt you provided they contain no more than those commonly used." Then she went on to admonish him, saying, "Have a care; stay at the third glass; I consider you have an obligation to strict temperance, which all have not; I mean your designation to holy orders. Remember, under the Jewish economy it was ordained by God himself that the snuffers of the temple should be perfect gold; for which we may infer that those who are admitted to serve at the altar . . . ought themselves to be most pure, and free from scandalous action. . . ."[13]

Apparently, Susanna had a concern for Sammy's salvation because seemingly she wrote to him more often than the other boys, instructing him on how to walk with God. In one letter to him she instructed him on how to be saved. (So even though there has been controversy about when she herself was saved, she demonstrates a concern for the lost, which is typically not something an unbeliever would care about.) But, in her letter she used terminology that could be seen to show that she was not as clear as she could be about the way of salvation:

> This life is nothing in comparison of eternity; so very inconsiderable, and withal so wretched, it is not worthwhile to be, if we were to die as the beasts. What mortal would sustain the pains the once, the disappointments, the cares and thousands of calamities we must often suffer here? But when we consider this as a probationary state. . . . and that if we wisely behave ourselves here, if we purify ourselves from all corrupt and inordinate affections, if we can, by the divine assistance, recover the image of God (moral goodness) which we lost in Adam, and attained to a heavenly temper and disposition of mind, full of the love of God, etc. then we justly think that this life is an effect of the inconceivable goodness of God towards us. . . .

> I have such a vast inexpressible desire of your salvation, and such dreadful apprehensions of your failing in a work of so great importance; and do moreover know by experience how hard a thing it is to be a Christian, that I cannot for fear, I cannot but most earnestly press you and conjure you, over and over again to give the most earnest heed to what you have already learned, lest at any time you let slip the remembrance of your final happiness, or forget what you have to do in order to attain it.[14]

This quote from Susanna is both troubling and confusing for a number of reasons:

- Susanna considers that this life is a "probationary state." Normally, being on probation implies the avoidance of punishment or imprisonment by means of good behavior (works). However, Scripture says that we must be saved by faith, not our own good works (see Ephesians 2:8).

- Further, she said, ". . . if we behave wisely here," which shows she was hoping that her good deeds would save her.

- She adds, ". . . if we purify our souls." How is that possible? Only God can do that. Scripture tells us that we need the "washing of regeneration, and renewing of the Holy Ghost" (Titus 3:5).

- She wrote: "I have such a vast inexpressible desire of your salvation, and such dreadful apprehensions of your failing in a work of so great importance," and "how hard a thing it is to be a Christian." This seems to underline the idea of working for salvation.

- Finally, she says that Sammy must not forget what he has "to do in order to attain it." It's unclear whether she is meaning a happiness or salvation. Either way using the word "attain" is a confusing word choice.

Arnold Dallimore explores Susanna's underlying assumptions when he writes:

As much as we may rejoice in the extraordinary earnestness manifested by Susanna in seeking Sammy's salvation, we cannot but regret that she did not know the "finished" work of Christ, and the assurance of salvation which God grants to "him that believeth." How different was this concept of Susanna's from that experienced by Charles and John following their conversion in May 1738!

It is evident that Susanna, holding so strongly to the doctrine of salvation by works, and depending on human reason rather than on divine revelation, would have rejected the teaching that man's salvation begins with God. This rejection she had taught to her children. John wrote to her on this matter when he was preparing for ordination. He confessed that he could not accept the seventeenth section of the *Articles of Religion*, which so plainly declares the Church of England's belief in the doctrine of predestination and shows it to be a beautiful and comforting doctrine.

Susanna replied to John, but she did not deal with predestination as presented in the Prayer Book. She dealt with it only in an exceptionally extreme and distorted sense, and nowhere did she refer to the several Scriptures that declare the doctrine nor did she treat of what was stated in the Article. Three of her letters to him reveal her views on this subject. In the first she says, "The case stands thus: this life is a probation, wherein eternal happiness or misery are proposed to our choice; the one as a reward of a virtuous, the other as the consequence of a vicious life."

In the second letter she asserts, "I do firmly believe that God from all eternity hath elected some to everlasting life, but then I humbly conceive that this election is founded in his fore-

> ## The Fruit of Salvation
> Do all the good you can, by all the means you can, in all the ways you can, in all the places you can, to all the people you can, as long as you ever can.
> —John Wesley

knowledge, according to Romans 8:29, 30." She then cites these two verses, assuming that God "foreknew" that some men, when presented with the gospel, would accept it. Nowhere does she mention the truth that man is "dead in trespasses and sin"— that he could do nothing and that God "foreknew" what he himself would do. Nor does she show any understanding of the biblical use of the word "foreknowledge" as a term indicating God's affection and love towards mankind.[15]

LETTERS TO CHILDREN

Susanna wrote another letter in 1727 to her son John Wesley, when he was twenty-four years old and a tutor at Oxford, where he was surrounded by many friends, including young women. She wrote to him about keeping a watch on his life. She wrote:

Ah, my dear son did you with me stand on the verge of life, and saw before your eyes a vast expanse, an unlimited duration of being, which you might shortly enter upon, you can't conceive how all the inadvertencies, mistakes and sins of youth would rise up to your view; and how different the sentiments of sensitive pleasures, the desire of sexes, the pernicious friendships of the world, would be then from what they are now, while health is entire and seems to promise many years of life.[16]

During this period of time, Susanna wrote not only to her children, but she also composed a manual for her children on Christian doctrine, as well as an exposition of the Apostles' Creed in which she explains it point by point.

Here we can see the nature of her expositions; this comes from a letter that she wrote to Charles after his conversion in 1738, regarding the passion of Christ and his suffering:

> He must be forsaken of his Father in the midst of his torments, which made him thrice so earnestly repeat his petition that if it were possible that cup might past from him. But the full complement of his sufferings we may suppose to be that he did at that time actually sustain the whole weight of that grief and sorrow which was due to the justice of God for the sins of the whole world. And this, we may believe, caused that inconceivable agony when his sweat was as great drops of blood falling down to the ground.

> And though his torments were so inexpressibly great, yet the Son of Man must suffer many things. He must be betrayed by one disciple, denied by another, and forsaken by all. And as he had suffered

SUSANNA WESLEY: *HER REMARKABLE LIFE*

in his soul by the most intense grief and anguish, so he had to suffer in his body the greatest bitterness of corporeal pains, which the malice and rage of his enemies could inflict upon it. And now the Sovereign Lord and Judge of all men is haled before the tribunal of his sinful creatures: the pure and unspotted Son of God who could do no wrong, neither could guile be found in his mouth, accused by his presumptuous slaves of no less a crime than blasphemy. . . .

But though the corporeal pains occasioned by the thorns, the scourging, by the piercing those nervous and most sensible parts of his most sacred body, were wrought up to an inexpressible degree of torture; yet were they infinitely surpassed by the anguish of his soul when there was (but after what manner we cannot conceive a sensible withdrawing of the comfortable presence of Deity, which caused that loud and impassioned exclamation: "My God, my God, why hast thou forsaken me?"[17]

Susanna's husband Samuel often wrote to Charles while he was away. In one of his letters he praised Susanna as being a great mother and how she had, despite suffering from so many sicknesses, continued to educate them and care for them:

> The true believer brings forth the fruit of a new lifestyle, a lifestyle that is pleasing in the sight of Almighty God. If we are rooted and grounded in Christ, it should be evident. Jesus said, "I am the vine, ye are the branches: He that abideth in me, and I in him, the same bringeth forth much fruit: for without me ye can do nothing" (John 15:5).

You know what you owe to one of the best of mothers. . . . Often reflect on the tender and peculiar love which your mother has always expressed towards you, the deep affliction, both of body and mind, which she underwent for you, both before and after your birth; the particular care she took of your education when she struggled with so many pains and infirmities; and, above all, the wholesome and sweet motherly advice and counsel which she has often given you to fear God, to take care of your soul, as well as your learning, to shun all vicious practices and bad examples . . . as well as those valuable letters she wrote to you.

You will not forget to evidence this by supporting and comforting her in her age . . . and doing nothing which may justly displease and grieve her, or show you unworthy of such a mother. . . .

In short, reverence and love her as much as you will. . . . For though I should be jealous of any other rival in your heart, yet I will not be of her: the more duty you pay her and the more frequently and kindly you write to her, the more will you please your affectionate father,

Samuel Wesley[18]

Charles took this advice to heart, as did John and the others. John conducted his mother's funeral service in 1742, by then having had assurance of her salvation. Charles wrote the epitaph for the tombstone. In part, it read:

SUSANNA WESLEY
1669–1742

A Christian here her flesh laid down,

the cross exchanging for a crown.

True daughter of affliction, she,

inured to pain and misery. . . .

The Father then revealed his Son;

him in the broken bread made known;

She knew and felt her sins forgiven,

and found the earnest of her heaven.[19]

CHAPTER 8
THE DEATH OF SAMUEL WESLEY

S AMUEL WESLEY, Susanna's husband, went to be with the Lord on April 25, 1735 at the age of seventy-three, which was considered old in the eighteenth century. His son Charles reported, "He was very, very frugal, yet decently, buried in the churchyard." This was the churchyard of the church where he had served for thirty-eight years of his life.

For as many as twenty-five years before his death, he had been working on his scholarly commentary on the book of Job, in hopes of making enough money to pay off his debts. He never succeeded. Ten years before his death, he wrote to his son John several times, lamenting his financial struggles. Here is a portion of one of these letters:

Bawtry, September 1st, 1725

Dear Son,

I came hither today because I cannot be at rest till I make you easier. I could not possibly manufacture any money for you here sooner than next Saturday. On Monday I . . . will try to prevail with your brother to return you 8 with interest. I will assist you in your charges for ordination though I am just now struggling for life. This 8 you may depend on the next week, or the week after.[1]

Approximately nine years before Samuel died, he suffered a stroke, which paralyzed his right hand. Surely

109

this slowed him even more in finishing his book on Job. Not only was he suffering physically, but Susanna was also unwell. In another letter to John, Samuel wrote, "You will find your mother much altered. I believe what would kill a cat has almost killed her. I have observed of late little convulsions in her frequently, which I don't like."[2]

When John and Charles read these sentences from their father they must have thought their mother was closer to death than she was. She would, in fact, live fifteen more years. During that time, Samuel employed John Whitelamb to help him finish his Job commentary, and also to assist him in other ways. In a letter to Susanna, Mr. Whitelamb described Samuel's attitude in his last days, saying:

> The constant struggling with my master's temper, which they only can have a just notion of who have been shut up with whole days in his study. . . . His satirical wit, especially in company, was more painful to me . . . If this would have been almost intolerable to another, much more to me who was conscious that I served him from a principle of generosity and love, and might have expected to be treated rather like a friend than one of the meanest of servants. The poor and wretched condition I was reduced to for want of clothes, so much worse than what I had been used to, and the universal contempt it exposed me to . . . and notwithstanding my silent tears and private mourning for my wretched state, yet I never ceased heartily to pray forth prosperity and health of the family.[3]

Samuel lived two years more after this, and then he had

another accident, which was more serious than any previous health issue. While traveling in a wagon, on Friday June 4, 1731, he fell out of the wagon. Susanna wrote to their son John about the incident:

July 12, 1731

Dear Jacky,

The particulars of your father's fall are as follows: On Friday, June 4th, I, your sister Martha, and our maid, were going in our waggon to see the ground we hire of Mrs. Knight. . . . He sat on a chair at one end of the waggon, I in another at the other end, Mattie between us, and the maid behind me. Just before we reached the close, going down a small hill, the horses took into a gallop and out flew your father and his chair. The maid seeing the horses run, hung all her weight on my chair, and kept me from keeping him company.

She cried out to William to stop the horses, and that her master was killed. The fellow leaped out of the seat and stayed the horses, then ran to Mr. Wesley, but ere he got to him, two neighbours. . . . raised his head, upon which he had pitched, and held him backward, by which means he began to respire; for it is certain, by the blackness of his face, that he had never drawn breath from the time of his fall till they helped him up.

By this time I was got to him, asked how he did and persuaded him to drink a little ale, for we had brought a bottle with us. He looked prodigiously wild, but began to speak, and told me he ailed nothing. I informed him of his fall. He said he knew nothing of any fall. He was as well as ever he was in his life.

We bound up his head, which was very much bruised, and helped him into the wagon again, and set him at the bottom of it, while I supported his head between my hands, and the man led the horses softly home. I sent presently for Mr. Harper who took a good quantity of blood from him; and then he began to feel pain in several parts, particularly in his side and shoulder. He had a very ill night, but, on Saturday morning Mr. Harper came again to see him, dressed his head, and gave him something which much abated the pain in his side.

We repeated the dose at bedtime, and, on Sunday he preached twice, and gave the Sacrament, which was too much for him to do, but nobody could persuade him from it. On Monday he was ill and slept almost all day. On Tuesday the gout came. . . . We thought at first the waggon had gone over him; but it only went over his gown sleeve, and the nails took a little skin off his knuckles, but did him no further hurt.[4]

By 1733, Samuel was well aware that he would not live much longer and he began to think deeply about who would take care of Susanna. He realized that he did not have a dime to his name or any possessions, so what would Susanna do once he was gone? He pleaded with his son Samuel to take over his position as Rector of Epworth, but Samuel, who felt more at home in the classroom than in the pulpit, declined.

Less than one year later, he offered the same position to son John. But John was comfortable in Oxford leading the Holy Club and rejected the offer as well. During 1734, Samuel got so sick that he was not able to preach, so he and Susanna wrote to John again, pleading with him for help, which made him have a change of heart. But unforeseen circumstances hindered him from coming after all, and he had to break the news to his sickly father.

In the early part of April, just before Samuel died, Susanna wrote to John and Charles pleading with them to come to Epworth to see their father right away. John tells about some of the last words that Samuel spoke before he departed to be with the Lord: "The inward witness, son, the inward witness, that is the proof, the strongest proof of Christianity."[5] John remarked that his father's last words showed that "The spirit of God bore an inward witness with his spirit that he was a child of God."[6]

Charles described their father's last day in great detail in a letter to his older brother Samuel. He wrote:

> The morning he was to communicate he was so exceeding weak and full of pain that he could not, without the utmost difficulty, receive the elements, often repeating, "Thou shakest me, thou shakest me"; but immediately after receiving there followed the most visible alteration. He appeared full of faith and peace. . . . The fear of death he had entirely conquered, and at last gave up his latest human desires of finishing Job, paying his debts, and seeing you. He often laid his hand upon my head and said, "Be steady. The Christian faith will surely revive in

this kingdom. You shall see it, though I shall not."[7]

As his adult children, John, Charles, Sukey, Emily, and his wife, Susanna, gathered around Samuel's bed, John asked him a pointed question as to whether or not he was near heaven. Charles recounts that he answered distinctly "and with the most of hope and triumph that could be expressed in sounds, 'Yes, I am.' He spoke once more just after my brother had used the commendatory prayer. His last words were 'Now you have done all.'"[8] And then he passed away.

CHAPTER 9
LIFE AFTER SAMUEL

THE DEATH OF SAMUEL was a major, life-altering event in many ways for Susanna, as they had been married for approximately forty-six years. She was used to living in the Epworth rectory, and now she was uprooted from there and would have to go from house to house, living with her children, for a period of seven years:

> She first stayed with Emily, now a schoolmistress in nearby Gainsborough. Then she moved southwest to live with Samuel, Jr., a headmaster in Tiverton, Devon, leaving him two years before his unexpected death in 1725 to be with her daughter Martha (called Patty) and her clergyman husband, Wesley Hall in three locations (Wooton, Wiltshire near Marlborough; Fisherton near Salisbury; and London). From that last brief arrangement it was an easy step to take up residence with her son John at his London headquarters, the Foundry, within haling distance of her birthplace."[1]

Interestingly enough, Susanna's communication with her friends expanded greatly, as she did a lot of letter writing during this season of her life. She apparently had more time on her hands now that her husband was gone and her children had grown up and built other relationships:

> Staying with her children in various corners of the land allowed her to make new friends, as far as we can tell from letters, all female. One such friend was Alice Peard, a woman she met while staying with

Samuel in Tiverton and wrote to at least once after joining Martha and Wesley Hall in Wiltshire. Another was the Countess of Huntingdon, an influential player in the evangelical revival who had sent her a bottle of Madeira and, apparently, a generous gift of financial support at the Foundry. If some of her new acquaintances were not up to that standard affability and/or generosity, that did not cause Susanna to pull back from contact in her advanced years.[2]

Her children supported her financially as she moved from one home to another, and she corresponded with them at length. Susanna wrote a series of letters to Charles in a two-year period from 1738 to 1739, and in these letters she asked for help financially and spiritually. She also expressed a longing to be visited by Charles and John (whom she very rarely saw). Once she wrote:

> **My Times Are in Thy Hand**
>
> My times are in thy hand;
> My God, I wish them there;
> My life, my friends, my soul I leave
> Entirely to thy care.
> My times are in thy hand;
> Whatever they may be;
> Pleasing or painful, dark or bright,
> As best may seem to Thee.
> My times are in thy hand;
> Why should I doubt or fear?
> My Father's hand will never cause
> His child a needless tear.
> My times are in thy hand,
> Jesus, the crucified!
> Those hands my cruel sins had pierced
> Are now my guard and guide.
> My times are in thy hand,
> I'll always trust in thee;
> And, after death, at thy right hand
> I shall forever be.
> —William F. Lloyd

My dear son Charles hath just been with me and much revived my spirits. Indeed I've often found that he never speaks in my hearing without my receiving some spiritual benefit: But his visits are seldom and short, for which I never blame him because I know he is well employed, and blessed by God, hath great success in his ministry.[3]

This gracious attitude of Susanna demonstrates her trust in God's sovereignty. She could have been more demanding of her sons' time, but "as out of the heart the mouth speaks", and she bore good fruit in these words to her sons. She had taken Psalm 31:15 to heart: "My times are in thy hand."

> Some have tried to deal with suffering by saying it's an illusion. Others have tried to deal with it by rejecting God. And others still have tried to deal with suffering by redefining God. Affliction is a reality in everyone's life at one time or another. . . . God does not suspend the laws of human nature and physical existence simply because we are redeemed.
> —Alistair Begg

The Lord is with us in the furnace, as He was with Daniel's three friends. They walked by faith and not by sight. Even when everything we hold dear gets stripped away "nothing will separate us from the love of God which is in Christ Jesus" (see Romans 8:35) Remember the fourth man who was in the furnace with Shadrach, Meshach and Abednego. That fourth man was Christ, and He did not remove them from the fire, but was with them in the fire. Psalm 23:4 says, "Even though I walk through the valley of the shadow of death I fear no evil for you are with me." God did not preserve them from the furnace, but he found them in it. He will always find us, regardless of what kind of trouble we are in. Even if the fire would have consumed them, a miracle still would have taken place that God changed their hearts so much they refused to worship a false god.

During her final years, in 1741, Susanna wrote an anonymous pamphlet defending her son John, who was in the midst of a public, theological disagreement with George Whitfield. Whitfield espoused the doctrine of predestination, which Wesley the Arminian disputed. In writing the defense, Susanna was able to express many of her gifts which had been previously suppressed:

First, it called on her adversarial personality, nurtured in puritanism, further cultivated in her nonjuring phase [the time when she refused to swear allegiance to King William], and continually reinforced in the struggles of her personal and devotional life. Second, it allowed her to demonstrate her intellectual acuity, to draw on her wide reading, and to employ the ready style she had developed in all her years as a closeted writer. Finally, public and private concerns coincided when she was able to identify her sons' cause with God's intention for the nation and defend them both. Though it might have been more gratifying to have her name on the pamphlet's title page, her anonymity seems appropriate; she had the quiet satisfaction of seeing her work in print and yet could assure herself that she was not transcending the boundaries of female modesty. And perhaps there was in addition, the canny realization that the work would be more effective if readers did not perceive it as a mother defending her son.[4]

LAST WORDS

Eventually, age caught up with Susanna. Before she lost her speech, her surviving daughters and sons gathered around her. She was able to address them for a final time:

> "Children, as soon as I am released, sing a psalm of praise to God," and they afterward obliged her. "An innumerable company of people" gathered for her funeral, John preached the sermon, and she was buried (appropriately, given both her origins and her own dissenting style, even as an Anglican) in the Dissenters' burial ground in Bunhill Fields just across from the future site of Wesley's City Road Chapel. Commented Wesley in his Journal, "It was one of the most solemn assemblies I ever saw, or expect to see on this side eternity."[5]

Of all of her children, she seems to have had the greatest impact on John Wesley, who later wrote, "If it were not unusual to apply such an epithet to a woman, I would not hesitate to say she was an able divine!"[6]

Depth of Mercy

Depth of mercy! Can there be
Mercy still reserved for me?
Can my God his wrath forbear,
Me, the chief of sinners, spare?
I have long withstood his grace,
Long provoked him to his face,
Would not hearken to his calls,
Grieved him by a thousand falls.
I my Master have denied,
I afresh have crucified,
Oft profaned his hallowed name,
Put him to an open shame.
There for me the Savior stands,
Shows his wounds and spreads his hands.
God is love! I know, I feel;
Jesus weeps and loves me still.
Now incline me to repent,
Let me now my sins lament,
Now my foul revolt deplore,
Weep, believe, and sin no more.

—Charles Wesley

CHAPTER 10

SONS OF SUSANNA: MUCH FRUIT AND REWARD

JOHN AND CHARLES WESLEY, the most famous of Susanna's surviving ten children, became fervent in their Christian faith. Both men were writers, and together they founded the Methodist movement with George Whitfield and others, which spread from England to the American colonies. Having been taught to read by their mother, Susanna, as soon as they could walk and talk, they had been educated rigorously regarding the things pertaining to godliness in living, and this bore much fruit throughout their lives as they preached about God, taught about disciplined living, and composed inspiring hymns.

As young men, John and Charles sailed to the American colonies, where they traveled to the colony of Georgia in British America. Their official duties for the governor and church varied, but both expected to help convert the native Indians to the faith. Charles was dispatched back to England before John was, but both men felt that their missions had failed.

On board the ship to the colonies, John had been faced with death when a violent storm arose, and yet a group of Moravian Christians on board the ship impressed him with their quiet faith. This caused him both to lack assurance that he was a child of God and to seek out the Moravians once his time in the colonies was over. He could see that his efforts to witness to others would be futile as long as he was unsure about his own salvation.

John wrote these telling words about his experience in Georgia in his journal on January 24, 1738: "I went to America to convert the Indians; but, oh, who shall convert me?" Continuing along these lines, he wrote:

> Who, what is he that will deliver me from this evil heart of mischief? I have a fair summer religion. I can talk well; nay, and believe myself, while no danger is near; but let death look me in the face, and my spirit is troubled. [Then] I have a sin of fear, that when I've spun my last thread, I shall perish on the shore! I think, verily, if the gospel be true, I am safe: for I not only have given, and do give, all my goods to feed the poor; I not only give my body to be burned, drowned, or whatever God shall appoint for me; but I follow after charity (though not as I ought, yet as I can), if haply I may attain it. But in a storm I think, 'What, if the gospel be not true?' Oh! who will deliver me from this fear of death? . . . Where shall I fly from it?'. . .
>
> February 1, 1738.

> This, then, have I learned in the ends of the earth, that I "am fallen short of the glory of God;" that my whole heart is "altogether corrupt and abominable;" . . . that my own works, my own sufferings, my own righteousness, are so far from reconciling me to an offended God, that the most specious of them need an atonement themselves; . . . that, "having the sentence of death" in my heart, . : . I have no hope . . . but that if I seek, I shall find Christ, and "be found in him, not having my own righteousness, but that which is

through the faith of Christ, the righteousness which is of God by faith. I want . . . that faith which enables every one that hath it to cry out, "I live not; . . . but Christ liveth in me; and the life which I now live, I live by faith in the Son of God, who loved me, and gave himself for me." I want that faith which none can have without knowing he hath it; [when] "the Spirit itself beareth witness with his spirit that he is a child of God."[1]

The Moravian's peace in the face of the storm on board the ship made a lasting impression on John. He found that they were as brave as they were gentle. Here is the direct account:

> One evening a storm burst just as the Germans began to sing a psalm, and the sea broke, split the mainsail in shreds, covered the ship, and poured in between the decks as if the great deep were swallowing them up. The English began to scream with terror, but the Germans calmly sang on. Wesley asked one of them afterward:
>
> "Were you not afraid?"
>
> "I thank God, no," was the reply.
>
> "But were not your women and children afraid?"
>
> "No," he replied mildly, "our women and children are not afraid to die."[2]

When the ship landed in Georgia after the stormy eight-week voyage, John became friends with a German Moravian pastor named Spangenberg, and he sought his advice:

"My brother, I must first ask you one or two questions: Have you the witness within yourself, does the Spirit of God witness with your spirit that you are a child of God?" Wesley knew not what to answer. The preacher, seeing his hesitation, asked: "Do you know Jesus Christ?"

"I know," said Wesley, "he is the Saviour of the world."

"True," replied he, "but do you know he has saved you?"

Wesley answered, "I hope he has died to save me."

Spangenberg only added, "Do you know yourself?"

"I do," was the reply; but in his Journal he wrote, "I fear they were vain words." Such a spiritual probing Wesley had never before received. The conversation was worth the journey across the ocean. The flash of lightning left him in darkness. He asked Spangenberg many questions about the Moravians of Herrnhut."[3]

I Felt My Heart Strangely Warmed

Back in England, the two brothers sought God earnestly even as they engaged once again in the religious endeavors they had initiated as part of their "Holy Club" at Oxford. Charles, through the faithful efforts of a new Moravian friend, came to a point of freedom in his faith a little earlier than his brother John did. Then came John's experience in a meeting at a house on Aldersgate Street in London on Wednesday, May 24, 1738:

In the evening I went very unwillingly to a society in Aldersgate Street, where one was reading Luther's preface to the Epistle to the Romans. About a quarter before nine, while he was describing the change which God works in the heart through faith in Christ, I felt my heart strangely warmed. I felt I did trust in Christ, Christ alone, for salvation; and an assurance was given me that He had taken away my sins, even mine, and saved me from the law of sin and death.

I began to pray with all my might for those who had in a more especial manner despitefully used me and persecuted me. I then testified openly to all there what I now first felt in my heart. But it was not long before the enemy suggested, "This cannot be faith; for where is thy joy?" Then was I taught that peace and victory over sin are essential to faith in the Captain of our salvation; but that, as to the transports of joy that usually attend the beginning of it, especially in those who have mourned deeply, God sometimes giveth, sometimes withholdeth them according to the counsels of His own will.

After my return home, I was much buffeted with temptations, but I cried out, and they fled away. They returned again and again. I as often lifted up my eyes, and He "sent me help from his holy place." And herein I found the difference between this and my former state chiefly consisted. I was striving, yea, fighting with all my might under the law, as well as under grace. But then I was sometimes, if not often, conquered; now, I was always conqueror.

Thursday, 25.—The moment I awakened, "Jesus, Master," was in my heart and in my mouth; and I found all my strength lay in keeping my eye fixed upon Him and my soul waiting on Him continually. Being again at St. Paul's in the afternoon, I could taste the good word of God in the anthem which began, "My song shall be always of the loving-kindness of the Lord: with my mouth will I ever be showing forth thy truth from one generation to another." Yet the enemy injected a fear, "If thou dost believe, why is there not a more sensible change?" I answered (yet not I), "That I know not. But, this I know, I have 'now peace with God.' And 'I sin not today, and Jesus my Master has forbidden me to take thought for the morrow.'"

Wednesday, June 7.—I determined, if God should permit, to retire for a short time into Germany. I had fully proposed, before I left Georgia, so to do if it should please God to bring me back to Europe. And I now clearly saw the time was come. My weak mind could not bear to be thus sawn asunder. And I hoped the conversing with those holy men who were themselves living witnesses of the full power of faith, and yet able to bear with those that are weak, would be a means, under God, of so establishing my soul that I might go on from faith to faith, and from "strength to strength."

[The next three months Wesley spent in Germany visiting the Moravians.][4]

The rest, as they say, is history. John and Charles

went on to found the Methodist movement, which had an enduring impact to this day, on both sides of the Atlantic Ocean and indeed, around the world. Having forced the matter, they nevertheless parted ways only reluctantly from the Church of England, in which they had been ordained; Charles never did sever his ties with that body. Charles wrote six thousand hymns, very many of which are still sung today (We have included the lyrics of a few of them). Their lives were never easy. In fact, their lives were much more difficult than they would have been had they remained in obscurity as their father had in his country parish.

To the credit of their mother and her unstinting efforts, they were able to combine their newfound power in the Holy Spirit with firm habits of disciplined, holy living that had been instilled into them in their childhood at the Epworth rectory.

Ho! Every One That Thirsts, Draw Nigh!

Ho! every one that thirsts, draw nigh!
('Tis God invites the fallen race)
Mercy and free salvation buy;
Buy wine, and milk, and gospel grace.
Come to the living waters, come!
Sinners, obey your Maker's call;
Return, ye weary wanderers, home,
And find my grace is free for all.
See from the Rock a fountain rise!
For you in healing streams it rolls;
Money ye need not bring, nor price,
Ye labouring, burthened, thirsting souls.
Nothing ye in exchange shall give,
Leave all you have and are behind,
Frankly the gift of God receive,
Pardon and peace in Jesus find.
Why seek ye that which is not bread,
Nor can your hungry souls sustain?
On ashes, husks, and air ye feed;
Ye spend your little all in vain.
In search of empty joys below,
Ye toil with unavailing strife;
Whither, ah! whither would ye go?
I have the words of endless life.
Hearken to me with earnest care,
And freely eat substantial food,
The sweetness of my mercy share,
And taste that I alone am good.
I bid you all my goodness prove,
My promises for all are free,
Come, taste the manna of my love,
And let your souls delight in me.
Your willing ear and heart incline,
My words believingly receive;
Quickened your souls by faith divine
An everlasting life shall live.

—Charles Wesley

Weary Souls, Who Wander Wide

Weary souls, who wander wide
From the central point of bliss,
Turn to Jesus crucified,
Fly to those dear wounds of His:
Sink into the purple flood;
Rise into the life of God!
Find in Christ the way of peace,
Peace unspeakable, unknown;
By His pain He gives you ease,
Life by His expiring groan;
Rise, exalted by His fall,
Find in Christ your all in all.
O believe the record true,
God to you His Son hath give
Ye may now be happy too,
Find on earth the life of heaven,
Live the life of heaven above,
All the life of glorious love.
This the universal bliss,
Bliss for every soul designed,
God's original promise this,
God's great gift to all mankind:
Blest in Christ this moment be!
Blest to all eternity!
—Charles Wesley

Jesus, Lover of My Soul

Jesus, Lover of My Soul
Jesus, lover of my soul,
Let me to Thy bosom fly,
While the nearer waters roll,
While the tempest still is high.
Hide me, O my Savior, hide,
Till the storm of life is past;
Safe into the haven guide;
Oh, receive my soul at last.
Other refuge have I none;
Hangs my helpless soul on Thee;
Leave, ah! leave me not alone,
Still support and comfort me:
All my trust on Thee is stayed,
All my help from Thee I bring;
Cover my defenseless head
With the shadow of thy wing.
Wilt Thou not regard my call?
Wilt Thou not accept my prayer?
Lo! I sink, I faint, I fall—
Lo! on Thee I cast my care.
Reach me out Thy gracious hand!
While I of Thy strength receive,
Hoping against hope I stand,
Dying, and behold, I live.
Thou, O Christ art all I want;
More than all in thee I find;
Raise the fallen, cheer the faint,
Heal the sick, and lead the blind:
Just and holy is thy Name,
I am all unrighteousness;
False and full of sin I am,
Thou art full of truth and grace.
Plenteous grace with Thee is found,
Grace to cover all my sin;
Let the healing streams abound,
Make and keep me pure within:
Thou of life the fountain art,
Freely let me take of Thee:
Spring thou up within my heart,
Rise to all eternity.
—Charles Wesley

Father, Saviour of Mankind

Father, Saviour of mankind,
Who hast on me bestowed
An immortal soul, designed
To be the house of God;
Come, and now reside in me,
Never, never to remove;
Make me just and good, like thee,
And full of power and love.
Bid me in thy image rise,
A saint, a creature new,
True, and merciful, and wise,
And pure, and happy too.
This thy primitive design,
That I should in thee be blest,
Should within the arms divine
For ever, ever rest.
Let thy will on me be done;
Fulfil my heart's desire,
Thee to know and love alone,
And rise in raptures higher;
Thee, descending on a cloud,
When with ravished eyes I see,
Then I shall be filled with God
To all eternity!

—Charles Wesley

Come, Sinners, to the Gospel Feast

Come, sinners, to the gospel feast,
Let every soul be Jesu's guest;
Ye need not one be left behind,
For God hath bidden all mankind.
Sent by my Lord, on you I call,
The invitation is to *all:*
Come, all the world; come, sinner, thou!
All things in Christ are ready now.
Come, all ye souls by sin opprest,
Ye restless wanderers after rest,
Ye poor, and maimed, and halt, and blind,
In Christ a hearty welcome find.
Come, and partake the gospel feast;
Be saved from sin; in Jesus rest;
O taste the goodness of your God,
And eat his flesh, and drink his blood!
Ye vagrant souls, on you I call;
(O that my voice could reach you all!)
Ye all may now be justified,
Ye all may live, for Christ hath died.
My message as from God receive,
Ye all may come to Christ, and live;
O let his love your hearts constrain,
Nor suffer him to die in vain!
His love is mighty to compel;
His conquering love consent to feel,
Yield to his love's resistless power,
And fight against your God no more.
See him set forth before your eyes,
That precious, bleeding sacrifice!
His offered benefits embrace,
And freely now be saved by grace.
This is the time; no more delay!
This is the acceptable day,
Come in, this moment, at his call,
And live for him who died for all.
—Charles Wesley

Happy the Man That Finds the Grace

Happy the man that finds the grace,
The blessing of God's chosen race,
The wisdom coming from above,
The faith that sweetly works by love.
Happy beyond description he
Who knows, The Saviour died for me,
The gift unspeakable obtains,
And heavenly understanding gains.
Wisdom divine! Who tells the price
Of wisdom's costly merchandise
Wisdom to silver we prefer,
And gold is dross compared to her.
Her hands are filled with length of days,
True riches, and immortal praise,
Riches of Christ, on all bestowed,
And honour that descends from God.
To purest joys she all invites,
Chaste, holy, spiritual delights;
Her ways are ways of pleasantness,
And all her flowery paths are peace.
Happy the man who wisdom gains,
Thrice happy who his guest retains!
He owns, and shall for ever own,
Wisdom, and Christ, and heaven are one.
                              —Charles Wesley

Afterword
God Works In Mysterious Ways

Trisha Ramos

WHILE DOING RESEARCH for this book, I started having some very unusual health issues. One month before the manuscript was due to the publisher I had severe vertigo for nearly two weeks. One particular Saturday I only felt relief outside on a chair sitting "Indian style." I sat that way for nearly ten hours. I felt solace and stillness while reading the Word of God and studying about the life of Susanna Wesley. If you have ever battled with vertigo, you know how horrible and debilitating it is. At times I didn't think I would see the light of day.

In addition, the health and wellbeing of those associated with Living Waters and Ray Comfort's ministry have been under strain. First, my dear friend Liz, who works with Ray, fell down the stairs breaking her arm in several places. Then Jen, who is one of Ray's assistants, had a terrible car accident. Debbie, the wife of Danny, a brother who works for the ministry, had a bad fall, and Daniel Comfort, Ray's son, had surgery which got infected and required more surgery. I definitely was in good company during my afflictions.

One day a friend texted me saying, "Listen to Arturo Azurdia on the psalms. I think it will encourage you." Then she added, "Just type his name in a Google search and put 'A song of . . . '" I did just that and came across a very good message by him on the twenty-third psalm. It was so powerful that by the end of the message I was in tears as I was reminded of the goodness and kindness of the Lord. I decided to listen to another message by him called, "A Song of Revelation."

I was intrigued by the opening portion where Arturo talks about how, in a small London house on Brook Street, a servant sighs with resignation as he arranges a tray full of food that he is going to serve to a composer (his boss) in his bedroom. The servant is discouraged because he knows the meal that he has labored over will most likely not be eaten. For more than a week his employer, an eccentric composer, has been in his room hour after hour. The servant delivers supper and returns later to find the bowls and platters largely untouched. Arturo went on to say that the composer was George Frederick Handel and the piece he was working on was titled, *Messiah*.

Interestingly enough, just months before all of this, Handel had found himself drowning in debt and he was hopelessly depressed at the fact that his operas were going out of style. The performance halls were nearly empty and he was about to lose everything. But an unseen providence came his way when his friend Charles Jennens gave him lyrics and asked him to write music to them. He had handed him the lyrics to "Messiah," which begins with the story of salvation, starting with the coming of the Savior, and then ends with everybody around the throne, singing to the Lamb.

It seems that Deism had been starting to infiltrate the culture. People were beginning to be inclined to believe there is a Creator, but that He has removed Himself from the creation and is inactive; he is not involved with the lives of individuals. Charles Jennens, Handel's friend, had lost his brother to suicide after he had a correspondence with a Deist who made him doubt his faith. Charles was deeply burdened over this. As a result, he put together the lyrics for "Messiah." He wanted the song to be a defense for the Gospel in the face of Deism. He knew the way to infiltrate the culture was via the opera or oratorio (which was for them what our modern day theater is for us now).

The lyrics are taken entirely from Scripture. Not a word is Jennens' and not a word is Handel's. It consists of verses mostly drawn from the Old Testament book of Isaiah, and it is all about the coming Messiah. Christ is in all of Scripture and Jennens saw that. He saw Him on every page.

Handel became so engrossed in the project that he barely would stop to eat. He told his friend that he would be done with the project in one year, but to everyone's surprise, he completed the entire project in just twenty-four days.

Twenty-three days went by. On the twenty-fourth day, Handel's servant approached the door, and stopped dead in his tracks. When he walked into the room, he saw Handel in tears, sobbing. Handel looked up and said: "I did think I did see all Heaven before me, and the great God Himself seated on His throne, with his Company of Angels."

Studying all of this led me to look at the time that Handel was born. George Frederick Handel was born February 23, 1685 and died April 14, 1759. Then I realized that the life of Susanna Wesley—born January 20, 1669 and died July 23, 1742—overlapped his. And *Messiah* was written in 1741.

In 1737 Handel had had a stroke that he recovered from. *Messiah* was written four years after the stroke and just one year before Susanna died. There's a very good chance that she would have heard it performed in London. In fact, we know that during the Easter season in April 1742, *Messiah* premiered and, interestingly enough, Susanna's beloved son John did see an early performance. History reports that his brother Charles actually got to know Handel a bit before Handel died, and visited him in his London home on more than one occasion.

My dear friend, Sherry Pierce sent me a wonderful hymn in an email during a time when she was ill. I had shared with her a couple days before about the vertigo issue I was battling. She thought this particular hymn would minster to me as it had ministered to her. Little did Sherry know I had been studying the life of George Fredrick Handel and other musicians from this time period, as well as Susanna Wesley. When I looked at the hymn and saw who it was written by, I thought "There must be a connection to Susanna Wesley."

The hymn was written by Henry Lyte, and the music by Wolfgang Amadeus Mozart. From my research I already knew that Susanna's eldest son, Samuel Wesley, had become an acclaimed English organist and composer, And—because he was a contemporary of Mozart—he was called by some "The English Mozart"! Here is the hymn:

> Jesus, I my cross have taken,
> All to leave and follow Thee.
> Destitute, despised, forsaken,
> Thou from hence my all shall be.
> Perish every fond ambition,
> All I've sought or hoped or known.
> Yet how rich is my condition!

God and heaven are still my own.
Let the world despise and leave me,
They have left my Savior, too.
Human hearts and looks deceive me;
Thou art not, like them, untrue.
O while thou dost smile upon me,
God of wisdom, love, and might,
Foes may hate and friends disown me,
Show thy face and all is bright.
Man may trouble and distress me,
'Twill but drive me to thy breast.
Life with trials hard may press me;
Heaven will bring me sweeter rest.
Oh, 'tis not in grief to harm me
While thy love is left to me;
Oh, 'twere not in joy to charm me,
Were that joy unmixed with thee.
Go, then, earthly fame and treasure,
Come disaster, scorn and pain
In thy service, pain is pleasure,
With thy favor, loss is gain
I have called thee Abba Father,
I have stayed my heart on thee
Storms may howl, and clouds may gather;
All must work for good to me.
Soul, then know thy full salvation
Rise o'er sin and fear and care
Joy to find in every station,
Something still to do or bear.
Think what Spirit dwells within thee,
Think what Father's smiles are thine,

> Think that Jesus died to win thee,
> Child of heaven, canst thou repine.
> Haste thee on from grace to glory,
> Armed by faith, and winged by prayer.
> Heaven's eternal days before thee,
> God's own hand shall guide us there.
> Soon shall close thy earthly mission,
> Soon shall pass thy pilgrim days,
> Hope shall change to glad fruition,
> Faith to sight, and prayer to praise.

After I finished reading the lyrics, I realized I had heard it before, and that this is the song my husband Emilio plays in his office all the time, which is where I first heard it, in the wonderful rendition of the music group known as Indelible Grace.

The vertigo may have made me slow, but one truth remains, no matter where you are, no matter where you have been and no matter what is ahead of you, God holds today and tomorrow, and if you are His, He is holding you. And one day we will see Him as He is; with Susanna Wesley, this is my hope: "Beloved, now are we the sons of God, and it doth not yet appear what we shall be: but we know that, when he shall appear, we shall be like him; for we shall see him as he is" (1 John 3:2).

Puritan Thomas Boston wrote a book called *Human Nature in its Fourfold State,* which was about the subject of seeing Christ just as He is. Here is an excerpt about the joys that await believers in heaven:

> Then we shall behold him, who died for us,

that we might live forevermore; whose matchless love made Him swim the red sea of God's wrath, to make a path in the midst of it for us, by which we might pass safely to Canaan's Land: then we will see what a glorious one he was, who suffered all this for us; what entertainment he had in the upper house; what hallelujahs of angels could not hinder him to hear the groans of a perishing multitude on earth, and to come down for their help; and what a glory he laid aside for us. Then will we be more able to comprehend, with all saints, what is the breadth, and length, and depth, and heighth; and to know the love of Christ, which passeth knowledge,. . . .

When the saints shall remember, that the waters of wrath he was plunged into, are the wells of salvation, from whence they draw all their joy; that they have got the cup of salvation, in exchange of the cup of wrath his Father gave him to drink, which his sinless human nature shivered at: how will their hearts leap within them, burn with seraphic love, like coals of juniper, and the arch of heaven ring with their songs of salvation?

They will be happy in seeing the Father, Son, and Holy Ghost, (not with their bodily eyes, in respect of which God is invisible . . .) but with the eyes of their understanding, being blest with the most perfect, full, and clear knowledge of God and divine things, Which the creature is capable of. This is called, the *beatific vision,* and is the perfection of the understanding, the utmost term thereof. It is but an obscure delineation of the glory of God, that mortals can have on earth; a sight, as it were, of his back part. . . . But there they will see his face. . . . They shall see him in the fulness of his glory, and behold him fixedly; whereas it is but a passing view they can have of him here, We who are heirs of *God*, the great heritage—shall then enter into a full possession of our inheritance; and the Lord will open His treasures of goodness unto us, that our enjoyment may be full. We shall not be stinted to any measure—but the enjoyment shall go as far as our enlarged capacities can reach. We shall be fully satisfied, and perfectly blessed in the full enjoyment of divine goodness.

Their love to the Lord being purged from the dross of self-love, shall be most pure; so as they will love nothing but God, and in God. It shall be no more faint and languishing, but burn like coals of juniper. It will be a light without darkness, a flaming fire without Smoke. As the live coal, when all the moisture is gone out of it, is all fire, so will the saints be all love, when they come to the full enjoyment of God in heaven, by intuitive and experimental knowledge of him, by sight and full participation of the divine goodness. . . .

Their joy shall be pure and unmixed, without any dregs of sorrow: not slight and momentary, but solid and everlasting, without interruption. They will enter into joy. . . . "In thy presence is fulness of joy," Psalm xvi. 11.[1]

PATH OF AFFLICTIONS

The longer I walk with the Lord, the more I am becoming aware of the afflictions of other believers, both living and now gone, such as Susanna Wesley and the Puritans, who all sought the comfort that only the Lord can supply.

One such living legacy is Jerry Bridges. I learned of his story after a friend handed me a book by him called, *Trusting God.* I received it while I was in the middle of battling vertigo and researching for this book. In the very first paragraph, Bridges describes how he lost his mom suddenly and unexpectedly when he was just fourteen years old. He heard her yell out from the room next to him, and then saw her take her last breath. His dad was so stricken with grief that Bridges had to handle his mom's death alone. He also talks about how it's been a long and difficult journey to learn how to trust God in the midst of frowning providences and times of affliction.

While reading about Bridge's afflictions, I learned about my friend Liz's terrible fall at Living Waters. Earlier in the evening, I had booked a flight for her to come and spend time with me while my husband was away at a conference in California. But that trip wasn't meant to be; she smashed her face on the stairs, breaking her nose, and broke her arm in several places. She had to be taken away in an ambulance.

Later in the evening, I was thinking about Liz and our afflictions and how they can cause irrational fears and panic attacks, so I picked up Ray Comfort's book called *Panic Attacks,* which is a terrific little book on overcoming and dealing with irrational fears. In addition to vertigo I had been struggling with heart palpitations, which has made me feel very out of control. Some nights I lose sleep over it, afraid that I won't wake up. I grab my Bible, journal and about ten different books and get on my knees to seek the Lord, hoping the palpitations will cease.

Just before I picked up *Panic Attacks*, I was telling my husband, Emilio that it bothers me when my heart does the fluttering routine. I feel the need to cough, because it reminds me of how our dog, Baby, died. She would have fast heart beats and weird rhythms and it would make her cough. That thought began to plague my mind. I expressed that concern to Emilio to which he wisely said, "Don't compare yourself to a dog."

I started to read Ray's book where I had left off, which was just as he was writing about a dark time in Charles Spurgeon's life. It included this quote from Spurgeon:

> I had almost lost my reason for some three weeks, and was desponding and brokenhearted. I was alone, walking in solitude, mourning, and weeping as I did day and night, and all of a sudden there came into my mind as though it dropped from heaven, this text: "Him has God highly exalted and given Him a name which is above every name that at the name of Jesus every knee should bow."

The thought that crossed my mind was this: I am one of his soldiers, and I am lying in a ditch to die. It doesn't matter; the King has won the victory. Christ has won the victory. . . . If I die like a dog, I care not. The crown is on His head. He is safely exalted.

I read it to Emilio and he laughed out loud and so did I. Leave it to Spurgeon to be so blunt: "If I die like a dog, I care not." It didn't matter how he died. He knew that death was his gateway to glory. He must die in order to see the King. The apostle Paul knew this, too:

> Who shall separate us from the love of Christ? shall tribulation, or distress, or persecution, or famine, or nakedness, or peril, or sword? As it is written, For thy sake we are killed all the day long; we are accounted as sheep for the slaughter. Nay, in all these things we are more than conquerors through him that loved us. For I am persuaded, that neither death, nor life, nor angels, nor principalities, nor powers, nor things present, nor things to come, Nor height, nor depth, nor any other creature, shall be able to separate us from the love of God, which is in Christ Jesus our Lord. (Romans 8:35–39)

What stood out to me, in a way that I had never seen before, was that he puts "death" as the very first thing on his list of ten things. He could have put it in the middle or at the end but my suspicion is that it was the first thing on his mind and perhaps he knew it was first on the mind of the believers. Maybe they were being tormented by the fear of death. They knew that persecution would come for following Christ. So he tells them not even *death* can separate them from the love of God.

THE PATH LEADS TO GLORY

Where you go after you die? Where will you spend eternity when your life here on earth is over?

Statistically, as you must know, nine people out of nine people die! That means you won't escape death. No one will. And eternity is a long time. It is forever. It never ends. There is nothing more important to be sure of than where you will be going after you die.

Have you ever stopped to look at yourself according to how God sees you? If not, here is how you can do it. Evaluate yourself by the Ten Commandments to see how you measure up to God's standard of righteousness:

1. Have you ever lied (even once—fibs, white lies, etc.)?

2. Have you ever stolen something (the value of what you stole is irrelevant)?

3. Have you ever looked with lust? Jesus said, "Whoever looks upon a woman to lust after her, has committed adultery already with her in his heart" (see Matthew 5:27–28).

If you have said "Yes" to these three questions' then (by your own admission) you are a lying, thieving, adulterer at heart—and we've only looked at three of the Ten Commandments. Here is another one of them:

Have you put God first in your life? (Or have you created a false god to suit yourself; a god you feel comfortable with?) If God judges you regarding who or what you have set up as god instead of Him, do you think you will be innocent or guilty on the Day of Judgment? If you're honest and listen to your conscience you know that you will be guilty, and end up in Hell. The reality of that should strike terror in your heart!

But wait . . . there's Good News!

God Himself made a way (the only way) for sinners to be forgiven: "For God so loved the world, that he gave his only begotten Son, that whosoever believeth in him should not perish, but have everlasting life" (John 3:16). Jesus Christ was fully God and fully man and was without sin. He suffered and died on the cross and then He rose from the dead, defeating death. You broke the Law and Jesus paid the fine with His precious blood for sinners! Today, here's what to do, confess your sins to God, repent (turn) from your sins, put your trust in Jesus to save you from eternal damnation, and you will pass from death to life. Only through Christ can God forgive you and grant you the gift of everlasting life.

I titled this Afterword "God Works in Mysterious Ways," because He does. There is a hymn about that very topic written by William Cowper in 1773. Cowper was a contemporary of Susanna Wesley. This hymn is reportedly the last one that he ever wrote, and Cowper, who often struggled with serious depression, wrote it after God had resolved a crisis in his life. Here is what happened:

> One night he [Cowper] decided to commit suicide by drowning himself. He called a cab and told the driver to take him to the Thames River. However, thick fog came down and prevented them from finding the river (another version of the story has the driver getting lost deliberately). After driving around lost for a while, the cabby finally stopped and let Cowper out. To Cowper's surprise, he found himself on his own doorstep: God had sent the fog to keep him from killing himself."[2]

Here is Cowper's hymn:

> God Moves in a Mysterious Way
> God moves in a mysterious way
> His wonders to perform;
> He plants His footsteps in the sea
> And rides upon the storm.
> Deep in unfathomable mines
> Of never failing skill
> He treasures up His bright designs
> And works His sovereign will.
> Ye fearful saints, fresh courage take;
> The clouds ye so much dread
> Are big with mercy and shall break
> In blessings on your head.
> Judge not the Lord by feeble sense,
> But trust Him for His grace;
> Behind a frowning providence
> He hides a smiling face.
> His purposes will ripen fast,
> Unfolding every hour;
> The bud may have a bitter taste,
> But sweet will be the flower.
> Blind unbelief is sure to err
> And scan His work in vain;
> God is His own interpreter,
> And He will make it plain.[3]

If you are in Christ you don't have to fear. You are in the safest place possible. Every fall down the stairs, He sees. Every heart palpitation, He holds in His hands. Every seemingly negative trial, He will make good. He will use every difficult circumstance for your good and His glory (see Romans 8:28). Every child Susanna lost, He was there, every fire she went through He used for her good and for the furthering of the gospel.

Christ has conquered the grave, and death will one day be swallowed up in victory (see 1 Corinthians 15:54). That should give you reason to rejoice today.

Notes

A Word to the Reader

1. Arthur Bennet, ed., *The Valley of Vision: A Collection of Puritan Prayers and Devotions* (Edinburgh, Scotland: Banner of Truth Trust, 1975).

Chapter 1:
Life Growing Up for Susanna

1. John Kirk, *The Mother of the Wesleys: A Biography* (London: Forgotten Books, 2012), 23. Original work published in 1866.

2. Arnold A. Dallimore, *Susanna Wesley* (Grand Rapids, Mich.: Baker, 1993), 11.

3. Sandy Dengler, *Susanna Wesley, Servant of God* (Chicago, Moody, 1987), 8. (This book is a biography of Susanna Wesley written for children. The author has invented dialogue based on actual facts.)

4. Dengler, 9.

5. Dengler, 10.

6. Kirk, 37.

7. Dallimore, 13.

8. Kirk, 42–43.

9. Dengler, 13.

10. Kirk, 5.

11. Kirk, 12

12. Dallimore, 12.

13. Dallimore, 12–13.

14. George J. Stevenson, *Memorials of the Wesley Family* (New York: Partridge & Co., 1876), 160.

15. Dallimore, 15.

16. Kirk, 10.

17. Dallimore, 15.

CHAPTER 2:
PURITANS IN HER HOME

1. From "The Third Foreword: Addressed to the Christian Reader," in *The Works of Elisha Coles (1608–1688)* http://www.pbministries.org/Theology/Elisha%20Coles/Severegnity%20of%20God/forward-3.htm.

2. As quoted on "Awake and Go: Global Prayer Network" (http://www.watchword.org/index.php?option=com_content&task=view&id=12&Itemid=31)

3. From *Fire and Ice: Puritan and Reformed Writings,* "How to Spend the Day with God," adapted and updated from Richard Baxter by Matthew Vogan (http://www.puritansermons.com/baxter/baxter5.htm)

4. Bennet, *The Valley of Vision.*

CHAPTER 3:
SUSANNA MEETS PRINCE CHARMING

1. Dallimore, 21.

2. Dallimore, 21–22.

3. Dallimore, 44–45.

4. Kirk, 45.

5. Dallimore, 22.

6. Dallimore, 22.

7. Dallimore, 22.

8. Dallimore, 23.

9. Dallimore, 24.

10. Dallimore, 26.

11. Dallimore, 31.

12. Dallimore, 31.

13. "Susanna Wesley," *History's Women Newsletter* (http://www.historyswomen.com/womenoffaith/ SusannahWesley.html).

14. http://www.historyswomen.com/womenoffaith/ SusannahWesley.html

15. The life and times of the Rev. John Wesley, M.A., Tyerman, Luke. Page 81-2

16. Luke Tyerman, *The Life and Times of the Rev. John Wesley, M.A., Founder of the Methodists* (London: Hodder and Stoughton, 1871), 127.

17. Dallimore, 35.

18. Dallimore, 35.

19. Kirk, 66–67.

20. Kirk, 68.

CHAPTER 4:
SUSANNA'S VIEWS ON RAISING GODLY CHILDREN

1. As quoted in "God's Pattern for Parents," John MacArthur, *Grace to You* website (http://www.gty.org/resources/print/sermons/1950B).

2. Henry D. Rack, 'Wesley, Samuel the younger (1690/91–1739)', *Oxford Dictionary of National Biography* (Oxford: Oxford University Press, 2004

3. From "John and Charles Wesley," *My Methodist History: Telling the Story of the People Called Methodist,* (http://www.mymethodisthistory.org.uk/page_id__384_path__0p3p131p.aspx).

4. "John Wesley," *Wikipedia* (http://en.wikipedia.org/wiki/John_Wesley)5. From "Faith of our Mothers," cached on website *Sermons.logos.com* (https://sermons.logos.com/submissions/70228-sf832-FAITH-OF-OUR-MOTHERS-2-Timothy-1-3-5-#content=/submissions/70228

5. Dallimore, 31.

6. See chapter 5.

7. Dallimore, 57.

8. Dallimore, 57–58.

9. Kirk, 136–137.

10. Kirk, 137.

11. Kirk, 137.

12. Dallimore, 60.

13. Dallimore, 61.

14. Eliza Clarke, *Famous Women: Susanna Wesley* (London: W.H. Allen & Co., 1886), 52. (Scanned and archived online at http://www.archive.org/stream/

susannawesley00clariala/susannawesley00clariala_
djvu.txt)

15. Kirk, 178.

16. "16 House Rules by Susannah Wesley, Raising
Godly Children, (http://www.raisinggodlychildren.
org/2011/03/16-house-rules-by-susannah-wesley-john.
html)

17. "16 House Rules by Susannah Wesley," *Raising
Godly Children,* (http://www.raisinggodlychildren.
org/2011/03/16-house-rules-by-susannah-wesley-john.
html)

18. "Conquer the Child's Will," *Journal of John Wesley*
(http://www.ccel.org/ccel/wesley/journal.vi.iv.xx.html)

19. William Nicholson, "Divine Comfort!" (http://
gracegems.org/Nicholson/divine_comfort.htm).

20. Photo Credit: Will Grady

CHAPTER 5:
SUSANNA'S TRIUMPHS AND TRIALS

1. Kirk, 276.

2. Donald N. Bastian, "When Unsatisfactory Marriages
Are Made in Good Families" (http://justcallmepastor.
wordpress.com/tag/susanna-wesley/)

3. Bastian.

4. Dallimore, 47.

5. Dallimore, 47.

6. Dallimore, 53.

7. Clarke, 50–51.

8. Clarke, 51.

9. http://www.archive.org/stream/susannawesley00clariala/susannawesley00clariala_djvu.txt

10. Kirk, 135.

11. Clarke, 54.

12. Kirk, 93.

13. As quoted in "The Weaker We Feel, the Harder We Lean," Joni Eareckson Tada (http://www.joniandfriends.org/radio/5-minute/weaker-we-feel-harder-we-lean/)

14. *Susanna Wesley: The Complete Writings*. Charles Wallace, Jr., ed. (New York: Oxford University Press, 1997), 95.

15. Wallace, 210.

16. Anne Adams, "Susanna Wesley—Mother of Methodism," *History's Women Newsletter* (http://www.historyswomen.com/womenoffaith/susannahwesley.htm).

17. Dallimore, 156.

18. Adams.

19. From the pamphlet, *Hope . . . The Best of Things,* by Joni Eareckson Tada (Crossway, 2008).

20. Bennet, *Valley of Vision.*

CHAPTER 6:
SUSANNA'S RELIANCE ON PRAYER

1. *The Prayers of Susanna Wesley,* W.L Doughty, ed. (London: Epworth Press, 1956), 17.

2. From Mark Gilroy, *How Great Is Our God: Classic Writings from History's Greatest Christian Thinkers in Contemporary English* (Brentwood, Tenn.: Worthy Publishing, 2011), n.p.

3. Richard Baxter, *The Practical Works of Richard Baxter* (London: George Virtue, 1838), 24.

4. Richard Baxter, *The Saints' Everlasting Rest* (Glasgow: Wm. Collins, 1831), 417–446 (language has been modernized).

5. Sharon Glasgow, "Susanna Wesley's Prayer Apron," blog entry (http://sharonglasgow.com/2013/07/susanna-wesleys-prayer-apron-powerful-life-story).

6. Annie E. Keeling, *Susanna Wesley and other eminent Methodist women* (London: CH. Kelly, 1897), 33 (https://archive.org/stream/cu31924029471590#page/n33/mode/2up).

7. Donald L. Kline, *Susanna Wesley: God's Great Catalyst for Revival* (Lima, Ohio: C.S.S. Publishing, 1980), 51.

8. *Susanna Wesley: God's Catalyst for Revival*, Donald L. Kline, (Lima, OH: C.S.S. Publishing, 1980), 49.

9. Rebecca Lamar Harmon, *Susanna: Mother of the Wesleys* (New York: Abingdon, 1968), 766.

10. Kline, 42.

11. From *Fire and Ice: Puritan and Reformed Writings,* "How to Spend the Day with God," adapted and updated from Richard Baxter by Matthew Vogan (http://www.puritansermons.com/baxter/baxter5.htm)

12. Keeling, 23.

13. John Wesley, *The Heart of Wesley's Journal*, Percy Livingstone Parker, ed. (New York: Fleming H. Revell, 1903), 93–101.

14. Keeling, 33.

15. Clarke, 48–49.

16. Clarke, 226–227.

17. William Horton Foster, *Susannah Wesley: Heroines of Modern Religion*, Warren Dunham Foster, ed. (New York: Sturgis & Walton, 1913). Viewable online at http://www.path2prayer.com/article/1039/revival-and-holy-spirit/books-sermons/new-resources/famous-christians-books-and-sermons/susanna-wesley-mother-of-methodism/susanna-wesley-a-biography.

18. *A Golden Treasury of Puritan Quotations*, I.D.E. Thomas, ed., (Edinborough, Scotland: Banner of Truth Trust, 1977), 209–210.

19. Taken from *Hearts Aflame: Prayers of Susanna, John, and Charles Wesley,* Michael McMullen, ed. (London: Triangle Press, 1995).

20. Bennet, *Valley of Vision.*

CHAPTER 7:
SUSANNA'S CONVERSION— TRUE OR FALSE?

1. Wallace, 16.

2. Kirk, 241.

3. Kirk, 242.

4. Kirk, 244.

5. Kirk, 244.

6. Kirk, 244.

7. Kirk, 245–246.

8. Kirk, 240.

9. Dallimore, 90.

10. Kirk, 248.

11. Kirk, 249.

12. Dallimore, 91.

13. Wallace, 52–53.

14. Dallimore, 92.

15. Dallimore, 92–93.

16. George J. Stevenson, *Memorials of the Wesley Family* (London, S.W. Partridge, 1876), 204.

17. From the Proceedings of the Wesley Historical Society, 1898.

18. Stevenson, 101.

19. J.B. Wakeley, *Anecdotes of the Wesleys: Illustrative of Their Character and Personal History* (New York: Nelson & Phillips, 1869.

CHAPTER 8:
THE DEATH OF SAMUEL WESLEY

1. Stevenson, 123.

2. Stevenson, 128.

3. From page 129 of the Proceedings of the Wesley Historical Society, June 1960.

4. Stevenson, 134.

5. Dallimore, 152.

6. Tyerman, page 444

7. Dallimore, 152.

8. Dallimore, 152.

Chapter 9:
Life After Samuel

1. Wallace, 15.

2. Wallace, 15.

3. Wallace, 16.

4. Wallace, 17.

5. Wallace, 17.

6. Wallace, 16.

Chapter 10:
Sons of Susanna—
Much Fruit and Reward

1. From "To America and Back," Wesley Center online (http://wesley.nnu.edu/john-wesley/john-wesley-the-methodist/chapter-vi-to-america-and-back/), a reproduction of the book, *John Wesley the Methodist: A Plain Account of his Life and Work,* by a Methodist Preacher (New York: Methodist Book Concern, 1903).

2. From "To America and Back."

3. From "To America and Back."

4. *Journal of John Wesley* (http://www.ccel.org/ccel/wesley/journal.vi.ii.xvi.html)

5. Afterword

6. Thomas Boston, *Human Nature and its Fourfold State* (Boston: Thomas and Andrews, 1796), 377–380.

7. "William Cowper," on NetHymnal (http://www.cyberhymnal.org/htm/g/m/gmovesmw.htm).

8. "God Works in a Mysterious Way," NetHymnal (http://www.cyberhymnal.org/htm/g/m/gmovesmw.htm)

Famous Aethiests

by Ray Comfort

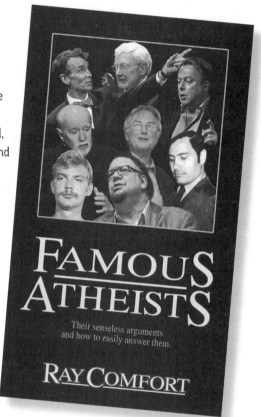

This publication looks closely at the beliefs of famous atheists, the lies they tell, arguments they make, and what they would have us believe about others who they say are and aren't atheists—such as Albert Einstein, Mark Twain, John Lennon, Steve Jobs, Brad Pitt, Hugh Hefner, Charles Darwin, Penn Jillette, Carl Sagan, Roger Ebert, Jim Jones, Jeffrey Dahmer, George Carlin, Bill Gates, Benjamin Franklin, Christopher Hitchens, James Cameron, Jodie Foster, Bill Nye, Billy Joel, and many more.

RAY COMFORT is a best-selling author of more than 70 books, including *The Evidence Bible* (a Gold Medallion Award finalist), and the co-host of "The Way of the Master," an award-winning television program seen in over 190 countries. He has spoken on the subject of atheism at Yale and other prestigious universities, debated atheism/evolution on ABC's "Nightline," and was a platform speaker at an American Atheists Inc. National Convention.

ISBN: 978-1-61036-134-7
MMP / 136 pages

Jaws Without Teeth
by Ray Comfort

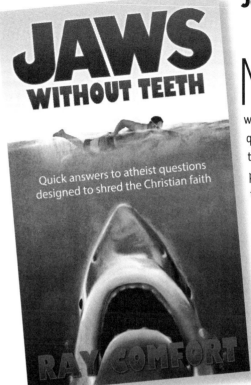

Many Christians are intimidated by atheists, whose carefully crafted questions are designed to rip Christianity in pieces and devour the faith. But a close look reveals that the atheist's arguments are toothless, as harmless as sharks that feed only on plankton. This brief book, in just a few sentences each, will give you concise, common-sense responses to those who embrace the foolishness of atheism and the unscientific and unobservable blind faith of evolution. The more than 200 questions and objections in this publication have been adapted from those asked by actual atheists.

RAY COMFORT is a best-selling author of more than 70 books, including *The Evidence Bible* (a Gold Medallion Award finalist), and the co-host of "The Way of the Master," an award-winning television program seen in over 190 countries. He has spoken on the subject of atheism at Yale and other prestigious universities, debated atheism/evolution on ABC's "Nightline," and was a platform speaker at an American Atheists Inc. National Convention.

ISBN: 978-1-61036-116-3
TPB / 144 pages

The Best of Ray

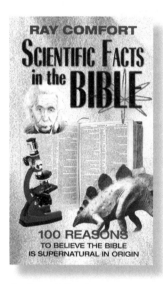

Scientific Facts in the Bible

Ray Comfort

Explore a wealth of incredible scientific, medical, and prophetic facts.

978-0-88270-879-9
MM / 104 pages

The Way of the Master

Ray Comfort and Kirk Cameron

A proven and effective way of making the gospel make sense to the unsaved. Learn how to speak directly to the conscience in the same way Jesus did.

978-0-88270-220-9
TPB / 368 pages

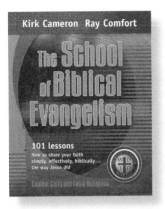

The School of Biblical Evangelism

Ray Comfort and Kirk Cameron

Learn how to share your faith simply, effectively, and biblically—the way Jesus did.

978-0-88270-968-0
TPB / 768 pages

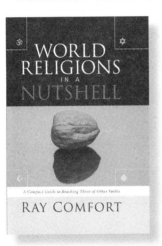

World Religions in a Nutshell

Ray Comfort

This book compares and contrasts Christianity with various religions . . . and includes sample witnessing conversations and testimonies of people from various faiths who have turned to Christ.

978-0-88270-669-6
HB / 208 pages

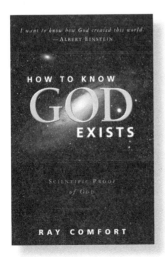

How to Know God Exists

Ray Comfort

The author, a noted evangelist, applies basic logic to three clear evidences for the existence of God. Uses scientific proof to show that God exists.

978-088270-432-6
TPB / 192 pages

Prayers
That Change Things

by Lloyd Hildebrand

More than 160,000 copies have been sold. These mass-market paperbacks contain prayers that are built from the promises of God and teaching that is thoroughly scriptural.

978-1-61036-105-7
MMP / 192 pages

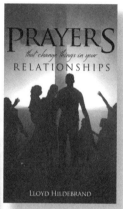

978-0-88270-012-0
MMP / 232 pages

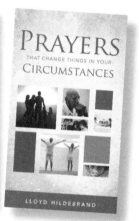

978-0-88270-743-3
MMP / 232 pages

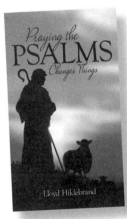

978-1-61036-126-2
MMP / 216 pages

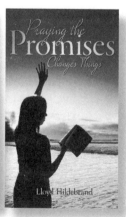

978-1-61036-132-3
MMP / 248 pages

978-1-61036-141-5
MMP / 256 pages